Mitchell Symons was born in London and educated at Mill Hill School and the LSE, where he studied law. Since leaving BBC TV, where he was a researcher and then a director, he has worked as a writer, broadcaster and journalist. He was a principal writer of early editions of the board game Trivial Pursuit and has devised many television formats. He is also the author of more than thirty books, and currently writes a weekly column for the *Sunday Express*.

Also by Mitchell Symons:

HOW TO AVOID A WOMBAT'S BUM

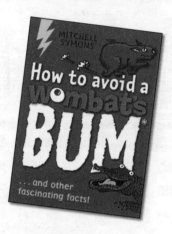

WHY EATING BOGEYS IS GOOD FOR YOU

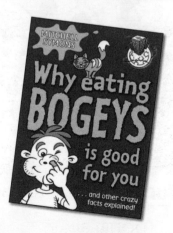

MITCHELL SYMONS

How much POO does an ELEPHANT do?

... and further fascinating facts!

DOUBLEDAY

HOW MUCH POO DOES AN ELEPHANT DO?
A DOUBLEDAY BOOK 978 0 385 61365 1

Published in Great Britain by Doubleday,
an imprint of Random House Children's Books
A Random House Group Company

This edition published 2008

5 7 9 10 8 6 4

Set in Optima

RANDOM HOUSE CHILDREN'S BOOKS
61–63 Uxbridge Road, London W5 5SA

www.kidsatrandomhouse.co.uk
www.rbooks.co.uk

Addresses for companies within
The Random House Group Limited can be found at:
www.randomhouse.co.uk/offices.htm

THE RANDOM HOUSE GROUP Limited Reg. No. 954009

A CIP catalogue record for this book is available from the British Library.

Printed and bound in Great Britain by Clays Ltd, St Ives plc

I dedicate this book to my wife Penny and my sons Jack and Charlie and also to you, the reader, because without you, I'd be talking to myself.

Acknowledgements

I've been collecting trivia facts all my
life. Where other lads would collect stamps, coins
and autographs, my idea of fun was finding out
extraordinary facts. Fortunately, I've never grown
out of my passion for the trivial, the bizarre and,
sometimes, the downright daft.

Two years ago I wrote a book – *How to
Avoid a Wombat's Bum* – choc-a-bloc full of facts
I'd amassed over the years and I was delighted
when thousands of people bought the book:
clearly, I'm not alone in
my enjoyment of fun facts.

Now I've written a follow-up which
I think is just as good than the original.
Dip into it anywhere you like (it is, after all, that
kind of book) and, hopefully, you
should find something to fascinate,
amuse or even astound you.

Now for some acknowledgements,
because without these people this book couldn't
have been written at all. In alphabetical order:
Luigi Bonomi, Lauren Buckland, Penny Chorlton,
Annie Eaton, Mari Roberts and Rhys Willson.

In addition, I'd also like to thank
the following people for their help, contributions
and/or support: Gilly Adams, Paul Donnelley,
Jonathan Fingerhut, Jenny Garrison, Bryn Musson,
Shannon Park, Nicholas Ridge, Charlie Symons,
Jack Symons, Louise Symons, David Thomas,
Martin Townsend and Rob Woolley.

If I've missed anyone out then please know that
– as with any mistakes in the book – it
is entirely down to my own stupidity.

Mitchell Symons
thatbook@mail.com

First things first

Orville Wright, the inventor (with his brother Wilbur) of the aeroplane, was involved in the first aircraft accident. His passenger, an American, was killed.

The first Englishman to be killed in an aviation accident was Charles Rolls of Rolls-Royce fame.

Thomas Jefferson grew the first tomatoes in the United States. He wanted to prove to Americans that they were not poisonous (as people believed).

The UK established the world's first speed limit. It was in 1903 and it was set at 20 mph (32 kph).

The first filmed sport was boxing in 1894.

Tradition says that the first member of a newlywed couple to buy a new item following the wedding will be the dominant force in the relationship. And so, to this day, some superstitious brides will arrange to buy a small item from one of the bridesmaids immediately after the ceremony.

Glenn Miller was the first recording artist or performer to receive a gold record. He received it for 'Chattanooga Choo Choo' in 1942.

Coca-Cola sold just 25 bottles in its first year.

In 1954 Richard Herrick received the first successful kidney transplant. It was donated by his twin brother, Ronald.

Sea sponges – which have a tough, flexible skeleton full of pores – were harvested as the first sponges used for bathing.

Neil Armstrong and Buzz Aldrin ate turkey in foil packets as the first meal on the moon.

Sunglasses first became popular in the 1920s, when movie stars began wearing them to counteract the photographers' bright lights.

The world's first cash dispenser was opened by British comedy actor Reg Varney at Barclays Bank, Enfield, London, in 1967.

The world's first scheduled passenger air service started in Florida in 1914.

The first supermarket in the world was in France.

The first word spoken by an ape in the movie Planet of the Apes was 'Smile'.

Ties were first worn in Croatia (which is why they were called cravats – *à la croate*).

The first police force was established in Paris in 1667.

The first Harley Davidson motorcycle was built in 1903 and used a tomato can as a carburettor.

The first ever CD single was Brothers in Arms by Dire Straits.

The first city in the world to have a population of over one million was London.

Construction workers' hard hats were first used in the building of the Hoover Dam in 1933.

The world's first traffic island was installed – at his own expense – by Colonel Pierrepoint outside his London club; he was killed crossing over to it.

In 1910 Harry Houdini became the first man to fly a plane in Australia.

Barbra Streisand is a multimillionaire singer and actress, but her first performance was as a chocolate-chip cookie.

The first duplicating machine was invented by James Watt, the inventor of the steam engine, in 1778 (patented in 1780) to help him with all the copying he had to do for his steam-engine business.

Britain's first National Lottery was in 1567 to pay for public works. The top prize was £5,000.

The first time rubber gloves were used by a surgeon was in 1890.

The first country to abolish capital punishment was Austria in 1787.

The Beatles' John Lennon's first girlfriend was named Thelma Pickles.

Britain's first escalator was installed in Harrods in 1878.

The world's first contact lenses were worn in 1930.

Uncle Tom's Cabin by Harriet Beecher Stowe was the first American novel to sell a million copies.

Pure trivia

There are 293 ways to make change for a dollar.

Walt Disney, the creator of Mickey Mouse, was afraid of mice.

If 20-a-day smokers inhaled a week's worth of nicotine, they would die instantly.

Watching TV uses up 50 per cent more calories than sleeping.

On average, a drop of Heinz tomato ketchup leaves the bottle at a speed of 25 miles (40 km) per year.

In 1994 an artist from Chicago called Dwight Kalb created a statue of the singer Madonna made from 80 kilos of ham.

Ben and Jerry's, the ice-cream makers, send their waste to local pig farmers to use as feed. Pigs love all the flavours except Mint Oreo.

The 19th-century French writer Guy de Maupassant hated the Eiffel Tower so much that he regularly used to eat lunch in the tower's restaurant – because that was the one place in Paris he wouldn't have to look at it.

'Mary, Mary, Quite Contrary' was based on Mary, Queen of Scots.

John Wilkes Booth assassinated Abraham Lincoln, but John Wilkes Booth's brother once saved the life of Abraham Lincoln's son.

King Mongut of Siam had 9,000 wives. Before dying, he was quoted as saying he only loved the first 700.

In Shakespeare's Antony and Cleopatra, Cleopatra plays billiards.

The woolly mammoth, extinct since the Ice Age, had tusks almost 5 metres long.

Henry I, King of England from 1100 to 1135, decreed that the distance between his nose and the tip of the index finger on his outstretched arm should be known as one yard (slightly shorter than a metre). He is also credited with creating the first zoo.

Microsoft once threatened a 17-year-old boy called Mike Rowe with a lawsuit after he launched a website called MikeRoweSoft.com.

Animals

Mice, whales, elephants, giraffes and humans all have seven neck vertebrae.

Squirrels can't see the colour red.

A bear has 42 teeth.

In India the term 'man-eating' is only applied to tigers that have killed three or more people. Ironically, man-eating tigers are usually too old to capture wild animals.

A group of 12 or more cows is called a flink.

A blind chameleon still changes colour to match his environment.

Mammals are the only animals with flaps round the ear holes.

African elephants only have four teeth to chew their food with.

The oldest breed of dog is the Saluki.

Armadillos have four babies at a time and they are always the same sex.

The antlers of a male moose are more than 2 metres across. A moose's antlers are made up of the fastest-growing cells in the animal kingdom.

A squirrel cannot contract or carry the rabies virus.

The sloth moves so slowly that green algae can grow undisturbed on its fur.

Emus can't walk backwards.

The giraffe has the highest blood pressure of any animal.

Gorillas sleep for up to 14 hours a day.

Camels are born without humps. Despite the hump, a camel's spine is straight.

During mating, the male Californian sea otter grips the nose of the female with his teeth.

Crocodiles carry their young in their mouths.

A hippopotamus is born under water.

Horses and rabbits can't vomit.

Every year in the US, more people are killed by deer than by any other animal.

Pumas can leap a distance of about 18 metres.

Celebrities who wrote children's books

Prince Charles	*The Old Man of Lochnagar*
Lenny Henry	*Charlie and the Big Chill*
Jamie Lee Curtis	*Where Do Balloons Go?*
Madonna	*The English Roses*
Sir Paul McCartney	*High in the Clouds: An Urban Furry Tail*
Billy Crystal	*I Already Know I Love You*
Jerry Seinfeld	*Halloween*
Ricky Gervais	*Flanimals*
Harry Hill	*Tim the Tiny Horse*
Will Smith	*Just the Two of Us*
LeAnn Rimes	*Jag*
Kylie Minogue	*The Showgirl Princess*
Katie Price (Jordan)	*Katie Price's Perfect Ponies*
Steven Gerrard	*Steven Gerrard: My Story*
Geri Halliwell	Ugenia Lavender

Notes sent by parents to school

Please excuse Joey on Friday; he had loose vowels.

Dear school: Please exkuse John for being absent on January 28, 29, 30, 31, 32 and 33.

Lillie was absent from school yesterday as she had a gang over.

Please excuse Johnnie for being. It was his father's fault.

I kept Billie home to do Christmas shopping because I didn't know what size she wears.

Please excuse Sara for being absent. She was sick and I had her shot.

Not what they seem

Catgut isn't made from cats, it's made from sheep.

Venetian blinds were invented in Japan, not Venice.

Camel-hair brushes are made from squirrel hair.

Soda water doesn't contain soda.

Turkish baths originated in ancient Rome, not in Turkey.

There wasn't a single pony in the Pony Express, only horses.

An ant lion is neither an ant nor a lion. (It is the larval form of the lacewing fly.)

Leaves don't change colour in autumn. They look green because they contain chlorophyll. When the leaf dies, the chlorophyll disappears and the other colours, which were there all along, emerge.

History

The only painting Vincent van Gogh sold in his lifetime was *The Red Vineyard*.

Spiral staircases in medieval castles ran clockwise so that attacking knights climbing the stairs couldn't use their right hands – their sword hands – while the defending knights, who were coming down, could. Left-handed men couldn't become knights.

The composer Ludwig van Beethoven was once arrested for being a tramp.

In ancient Greece women counted their age from the date they were married.

14 million people were killed in the First World War; 20 million died in the flu epidemic that followed it.

The shortest war in history was between Zanzibar and England in 1896: Zanzibar surrendered after 38 minutes.

The architect who built the Kremlin in Russia had his eyes gouged out by Ivan the Terrible so that he'd never be able to design another building like it.

In ancient Egypt priests plucked every hair from their bodies, including their eyebrows and eyelashes.

South American gauchos (cowboys) used to put raw steak under their saddles before starting a day's riding, to tenderize the meat.

Genghis Khan's cavalry rode female horses so soldiers could drink their milk.

Aztec emperor Montezuma had a nephew, Cuitlahac, whose name meant 'plenty of poo'.

Cleopatra used pomegranate seeds for lipstick.

Olive oil was once used for washing the body in Mediterranean countries.

The world's youngest parents were eight and nine, and lived in China in 1910.

In ancient China criminals who attacked travellers had their noses cut off.

To save money, Ben Jonson, Shakespeare's friend and fellow dramatist, was buried standing up in Westminister Abbey, London, in 1637.

Food and drink

During your lifetime you'll eat about 27,000 kilos of food.

The composer Beethoven was so particular about his coffee that he always counted out 60 beans for each cup.

M&Ms were developed so that soldiers could eat chocolate without getting their fingers sticky.

Watermelons, which are 92 per cent water, originated in the Kalahari desert in Africa.

Chocolate manufacturers use 40 per cent of the world's almonds and 20 per cent of the world's peanuts.

90 per cent of all new restaurants fail in the first year. Of the ones that survive, 90 per cent fail in the second year.

Sugar was added to chewing gum in 1869 – by a dentist.

Pork is the world's most widely eaten meat.

The world's costliest coffee is kopi luwak (civet coffee), which is produced from the droppings of an animal that eats only the very best coffee beans and then excretes them partially digested.

When it originally appeared in 1886, Coca-Cola was advertised as an 'Esteemed Brain Tonic and Intellectual Beverage'.

Milk chocolate was invented by Daniel Peter, who sold the concept to his neighbour, Henri Nestlé.

The tea bag was introduced in 1908 by Thomas Sullivan of New York.

Frederick the Great had his coffee made with champagne and a bit of mustard.

In the 1950s 80 per cent of chickens in Europe and the US were free-range. By 1980 it was only 1 per cent. Today the number has gone back up to about 13 per cent.

The French philosopher, Voltaire, drank 50 cups of coffee a day.

Lettuce is 97 per cent water.

Words

The word 'had' can be used eleven times in a row in the following sentence about two boys, John and Steve, who wrote similar sentences in their essays: *John, where Steve had had 'had', had had 'had had'; 'had had' had had the higher mark.*

The word 'and' can be used five times in a row in the following sentence about a sign being painted above a shop called Jones and Son: *Mr Jones looks at the sign and says to the painter, 'I would like bigger gaps between Jones and and, and and and Son.'*

The words loosen and unloosen mean the same thing.

'Hippopotomonstrosesquippedaliophobia' is the fear of long words.

The word 'coffee' came from the Arabic for 'excitement'.

The youngest letters in the English language are 'j', 'v' and 'w'.

No word in the English language rhymes with pint.

The magic word 'abracadabra' was originally intended for curing hay fever.

The word 'monosyllable', which means 'having one syllable', has five syllables.

The word 'starboard' is derived from the Old English word for the steering paddle on the right side of Viking ships: *steorbord*.

The longest English word that only uses the letters in the last half of the alphabet is 'non-supports'.

The longest word with horizontal symmetry (the top half is a mirror image of the bottom half) is COOKBOOK. It is only horizontally symmetrical when written in capitals.

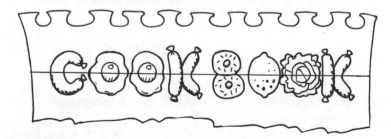

'Spoonfeed', nine letters long, is the longest word with its letters in reverse alphabetical order.

The word 'ushers' contains five personal pronouns spelled consecutively: he, her, hers, she and us.

'Rugged' and 'ague' are two-syllable words that can be turned into one-syllable words by the addition of two letters ('sh' to make shrugged; 'pl' to make plague).

'Are' and 'came' are one-syllable words that can be turned into three-syllable words by the addition of just one letter at the end ('a' to make area; 'o' to make cameo).

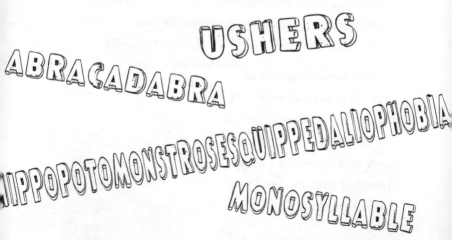

Babies

A newborn baby's head accounts for one-quarter of its weight.

When a baby is crawling, it balances on three 'feet'.

Paul Whitehouse won the Baby Smile of the Rhondda Valley award in 1963.

Newborn babies are given to the wrong mother 12 times a day in maternity wards across the world.

The ancient Greeks believed that boys developed in the right-hand side of the womb and girls in the left.

In the supermarket in the title sequence of The Simpsons, Maggie scans as $847.63. This was the average monthly cost of feeding and caring for an American baby.

Birds

The smallest bird in the world is the bee hummingbird: it's 5.7 cm long and weighs less than a tiny coin.

The pouch under a pelican's bill can hold more than 10 kilos of fish and water.

During heavy rain, turkeys look up and open their mouths, and some will drown.

Birds with the largest brains (relative to their size) have the best-developed immune systems.

The shell constitutes 12 per cent of an egg's weight.

The emu gets its name from the Portuguese word for ostrich.

An eagle can kill a young deer and fly away with it.

When the US air force was conducting test runs and breaking the sound barrier, fields of turkeys dropped dead.

Unlike humans, canaries can regenerate their brain cells.

Female canaries can't sing.

The ptarmigan, a brown bird, turns completely white in the winter.

The waste produced by one chicken in its lifetime could supply enough electricity to run a 100-watt bulb for five hours.

The hummingbird is the only bird that can fly backwards.

75 per cent of wild birds die before they reach six months old.

Percentage of bird species that mate for life: 90. Percentage of mammal species that mate for life: 3.

To keep cool, ostriches wee on their legs.

Fish

The red mullet only turns red after it's dead.

Many male fish blow bubbles when they want to mate.

The closest relative to the manatee is the elephant.

When young, black sea basses are mostly female, but at the age of five many become male.

The slowest fish is the seahorse, which moves along at about 0.01 mph.

The walking catfish can live on land.

A starfish can regrow an arm if one is torn off.

The electric eel is the most shocking creature on Earth. One zap from a 3-metre-long eel could stun a human. The larger the eel, the bigger the charge, and it can stun its victims from a distance of several metres.

The electric cells in an electric eel run up and down its tail. The eel uses its electric sense to 'see': the electric sensors send out impulses that bounce back off objects.

Unlike most fish, electric eels cannot get enough oxygen from water. Approximately every five minutes they must surface to breathe, or they will drown.

Many types of fish – called mouthbrooders – carry their eggs in their mouths until the babies hatch and can care for themselves.

Fish can taste with their fins and tail as well as their mouth.

To reach rivers and lakes where they spend most of their lives, many newborn eels swim nonstop for up to 3,000 miles (5,000 km).

The average cod deposits between 4 and 6 million eggs at a single spawning.

Sturgeon can live as long as 100 years. Mature females will produce millions of eggs every two to three years.

The African lungfish, which is a freshwater fish, can live without water. If there is a drought, it buries itself under a duvet of slime and earth, leaving a small opening to breathe. The earth dries and hardens, and the fish is protected. When it rains again, the earth dissolves and the lungfish swims away.

The flying fish builds up speed in the water then leaps into the air to escape predators. Once in the air, it can stay airborne for up to 100 metres.

Flatfish (halibut, flounder, turbot and sole) hatch like any other normal fish. But as they grow, they turn sideways and one eye moves round so they have two eyes on the side that faces up.

Minnows have teeth in their throats.

Saltwater fish, such as flounder and cod, have thicker bones than freshwater fish, such as catfish and trout.

Fish cough.

The human condition

If your body's natural defences failed, the bacteria in your gut would consume you within 48 hours, eating you from the inside out.

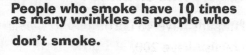

People who smoke have 10 times as many wrinkles as people who don't smoke.

Someone who eats little is said to eat like a bird – even though many birds eat twice their weight in a day.

The longest-recorded tapeworm found in the human body was 33 metres.

The Islands of Langerhans are a group of cells in the pancreas.

Not all our taste buds are on our tongue; about 10 per cent are on the palate and the cheeks.

Most people have lost 50 per cent of their taste buds by the time they reach 60.

15 million blood cells are produced and destroyed in the human body every second.

The surface area of a human lung is the same as that of a tennis court.

The opposite of 'cross-eyed' is 'wall-eyed'.

Humans have 46 chromosomes, peas have 14 and crayfish have 200.

Vegetarians live longer and have more stamina than meat-eaters, but they have a higher chance of getting blood disorders.

An eyelash lasts about five months.

On average, people can hold their breath for one minute. The world record is seven and a half minutes.

Over the last 150 years the average

height of people in wealthy countries has increased by 10 cm.

If the amount of water in your body is reduced by just 1 per cent, you'll feel thirsty.

On average a bout of hiccups lasts five minutes.

The bones in your body are not white – they range in colour from beige to light brown. The bones you see in museums are white because they have been boiled and cleaned.

We actually do not see with our eyes – we see with our brains. Basically the eyes are the cameras of the brain. One quarter of the brain is used to control the eyes.

In an average lifetime a person will walk the equivalent of three times around the world.

Every year 100 people choke to death on biros.

Only 30 per cent of humans can flare their nostrils.

Many more people can roll their tongue than cannot.

The USA

In Kentucky 50 per cent of people getting married for the first time are teenagers.

Tennessee has more neighbours than any other state in the US. It is bordered by eight states: Kentucky, Missouri, Arkansas, Mississippi, Alabama, Georgia, North Carolina and Virginia.

About 75 per cent of the people in the US live on 2 per cent of the land.

One out of five pieces of the world's garbage is generated in the United States.

Americans eat approximately 20 billion pickles every year.

Rhode Island is the smallest US state but it

has the longest official name: **Rhode Island and Providence Plantations.**

Maine is the toothpick capital of the world.

New Jersey has a spoon museum with over 5,400 spoons.

There was once a town in West Virginia called '6'.

The Bible is the most shoplifted book in the US.

60 per cent of all US potato products are made in Idaho.

50 per cent of Americans live within 50 miles of where they were born.

The city of Seattle, like Rome, was built on seven hills.

YOU ARE NOW ENTERING
6
PLEASE DRIVE CAREFULLY!

The geographical centre of North America is in North Dakota.

The highest point in Pennsylvania is lower than the lowest point in Colorado.

'Q' is the only letter that doesn't appear in the names of any of the 50 states.

Los Angeles's full name is: 'El Pueblo de Nuestra Señora la Reina de los Angeles de Poriuncula' and can be abbreviated to 3.63 per cent of its length: 'LA'.

There are more plastic flamingos in the US than real ones.

Point Roberts in Washington State is cut off from the rest of the state by British Columbia, Canada. In order to get to Point Roberts from any other part of the state, you have to go through Canadian and US customs.

30 per cent of all the non-biodegradable rubbish buried in American landfills is disposable nappies.

The average American chews 190 pieces of gum each year.

The city of Portland in the state of Oregon was named in a coin-toss in 1844. Heads Portland, tails Boston.

The way we live

62 per cent of British people speak no other language than English.

A third of British children have a personal computer in their bedroom.

People who work at night tend to weigh more than people who work during the day.

There's an average of 178 sesame seeds on a Big Mac bun.

The average person drinks 70,000 cups of coffee in a lifetime.

After a three-week holiday your IQ can drop by as much as 20 per cent.

The typical driver will honk their car horn 15,250 times during their lifetime.

Every year the average person eats 428 bugs by mistake.

Every year 8,000 people injure themselves while using a toothpick.

A typist's left hand does 56 per cent of the work.

The stall closest to the door in a public toilet is usually the cleanest, because it is usually the least used.

The average person spends two weeks over their lifetime waiting for the traffic lights to change.

Every year one ton of cement is poured for every man, woman and child in the world.

62 per cent of email is spam.

After hours working at a computer screen, look at a blank piece of white paper. It will probably appear pink.

Amusement park attendance goes up after a fatal accident. It seems that people want to take the same ride that killed someone.

Most digital alarm clocks ring in the key of B flat.

Car drivers tend to go faster when other cars are around. It doesn't matter where the other cars are – in front, behind or alongside.

Most toilets flush in E flat.

Wearing headphones for an hour increases the bacteria in your ear by 700 times.

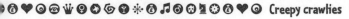

Creepy crawlies

Male ants develop from unfertilized eggs.
Queen and worker ants are developed from
fertilized eggs.

A snail breathes through its foot.

There are 3,000 types of lice.

**Scientists have performed brain surgery on
cockroaches.**

Moths can smell a single molecule.

Moths are not really attracted to light. Moths fly towards the blackest point, which is behind the light.

Cockroaches can detect movement as small as 2,000 times the diameter of a hydrogen atom.

The blood of insects is yellow. (The blood of mammals is red and the blood of lobsters is blue.)

The mayfly lives for one day.

Sanguinary ants raid the nests of other ant tribes, kill the queen and kidnap the workers.

The black widow spider can devour as many as 20 'mates' in a single day.

Bees are born fully grown.

The world's smallest winged insect is the Tanzanian parasitic wasp, which is smaller than a housefly's eye.

Blood-sucking hookworms inhabit 700 million people worldwide.

Only full-grown male crickets can chirp.

The largest insects that ever lived were giant dragonflies with wingspans of 91 cm.

The fastest Lepidoptera are the sphinx moths. They have been recorded at speeds of 37 mph (60 kph).

The pirate code

This varied from ship to ship but here, from the 18th century, is a fairly typical set of rules:

- Everyone shall obey orders.

- Booty shall be shared as follows: half goes to the captain, a quarter is shared by the gunner, boatswain and master carpenter, and the remaining quarter is divided among all the ordinary sailors.

- Anyone attempting to desert will be marooned. He will be left with a flask of gunpowder, a bottle of water and a gun with one bullet.

- The punishment for hitting a man is 40 lashes on the bare back.

- Failure to keep weapons clean will lead to the loss of a share of the booty.

- Everyone has a vote on all important decisions.

- Everyone gets a share of captured drink and fresh food.

- Anyone found stealing from another member of the crew will have his ears and nose split open and be set ashore.

- Gambling is forbidden.

- The penalty for bringing a woman aboard in disguise is death.

- No one may leave the crew until each man has made £1,100.

- The compensation for losing a limb is 800 silver dollars.

Pirates still exist. These days they use speedboats and carry automatic weapons but are just as merciless as the pirates of old. Most modern pirates operate in the China Sea or around the coasts of Africa and Brazil.

Bats

Bats, like people, usually give birth to one baby at a time. Twins are rare.

For their size, bats are the slowest reproducing mammals on Earth, giving birth to only one baby a year. This makes them vulnerable to extinction.

90 per cent of all bats in the world are tiny, and weigh less than 25 grams.

Vampire bats don't suck blood. They bite, then lick up the flow. They need about 2 tablespoonfuls of blood a day, which they can extract in about 20 minutes.

Bats are not blind, are far too smart ever to become entangled in human hair and seldom transmit diseases to other animals or humans.

Mexican free-tailed bats sometimes fly nearly 2 miles (3 km) high to feed or to catch tailwinds that carry them over long distances at speeds of almost 60 miles (100 km) an hour.

The leg bones of a bat are so thin that it cannot walk.

Bats are the only mammals that can fly. There is a 'flying squirrel', but it only glides on outstretched skin flaps.

The largest order of mammals, with about 1,700 species, is the rodent. Bats are second, with about 950 species.

Plants that are dependent on bats for pollination include dates, figs, cashews, avocados, cloves, mangoes, breadfruit, carob and almost every tropical night-blooming plant.

The giant bats called flying foxes, which live in Indonesia and elsewhere, have wingspans of almost 2 metres.

Celebrities and sports

Jason Statham was a diver who represented Great Britain in the Seoul Olympics.

Ryan Phillippe has a black belt in tae kwon do.

Nicole Richie was a very good figure skater and trained eight hours a day in an attempt to get into the American Olympic team.

Kate Bosworth was a champion equestrian and played varsity soccer and lacrosse.

Joely Richardson attended a Florida tennis academy for two years.

Lewis Hamilton gained his karate black belt at the age of 12.

James Alexandrou swam for his county and was ranked in the national top 10.

Martin Freeman was in the England junior squash squad.

Avril Lavigne was a top hockey player and earned Most Valuable Player honours two years running for her team in Ontario.

Ricky Tomlinson was offered a football trial by Scunthorpe United but didn't take it up.

Michael Parkinson was a good enough cricketer to play for Barnsley (with Dickie Bird and Geoffrey Boycott) and to have a trial for Yorkshire County Cricket Club.

Eminem is a keen darts player.

Sports

It takes 3,000 cows to supply the US national football league (NFL) with enough leather for a year's supply of footballs.

A bowling pin has to tilt just 7.5 degrees to fall down.

When Andy Murray was called up to play doubles for Great Britain's Davis Cup team in March 2005, he became Britain's youngest ever Davis Cup player.

Tennis started out in France, and its name is derived from the French for 'there you are' or 'take it'.

The (American) football huddle originated in the 19th century at Gallaudet University, Washington, DC, when the deaf football team found that opposing teams were reading their signed messages and intercepting plays.

All major league baseball umpires must wear black underwear (in case their black trousers split).

William Webb Ellis of Rugby School was credited with inventing the sport of rugby. It was another former pupil of Rugby, Tom Wills, who invented Australian Rules football.

There are two sports in which teams have to move backwards to win: tug-of-war and rowing. You can make that three if you include a backstroke relay race.

The goalkeeper of Turkish team Orduspor was given a £50 bonus in 1980 after his team lost 4–0. Normally he let in twice as many goals.

The average lifespan of a major league baseball is seven pitches.

A first-class soccer game has an average of 85 throw-ins – almost one a minute.

A Costa Rican worker making baseballs earns around $3,000 per annum. The average American pro baseball player earns around a thousand times that amount.

At one stage in the 1920s Chelsea had three players who were medical students.

Dartboards are made out of horsehair.

The Alexandra in Crewe Alexandra came from the name of the pub that hosted meetings to set up the club.

On the first day of the 1950–51 football season, all the promoted clubs lost, all the relegated clubs won and all the newly elected clubs drew.

In 1964, 350 football fans died in a riot after an equalizer by Peru was disallowed. The referee said afterwards, 'Anyone can make a mistake.'

Spurs didn't have a single player sent off in a Football League match between 1928 and 1965.

The 20 most visited countries in the world – in order

1. France
2. Spain
3. China (inc. Hong Kong)
4. US
5. Italy
6. UK
7. Austria
8. Mexico
9. Germany
10. Canada
11. Hungary
12. Greece
13. Poland
14. Turkey
15. Portugal
16. Malaysia
17. Thailand
18. The Netherlands
19. Russia
20. Sweden

Dame Ellen MacArthur

In 2005 Dame Ellen MacArthur sailed singlehandedly round the world in a record-breaking time.

She spent about two-thirds of her voyage down below in a custom-built living area that was 1.5 metres high and 2 metres wide. This area was kept deliberately small for safety reasons. In a compact space there was less risk of injury when she was thrown around by the elements.

She slept in short naps taken in regular snatches of five to eight minutes with some sleeps of 40 or 70 minutes.

To save weight, water wasn't stored on board but made from seawater via a device called a desalinator.

Ellen had to consume 5,000 calories per day to provide the necessary 'fuel' for her energy expenditure on the voyage. She ate mostly dried fruit snacks, muesli bars, crackers, oatcakes, crisps and chocolate.

Ellen MacArthur's Progress

She started saving school dinner money at the age of eight to buy her first boat.

She achieved her RYA Yachtmaster and Instructor's ticket at the exceptionally young age of 18.

In 1995 she won the BT/YJA Young Sailor of Year award and sailed her boat *Iduna* singlehanded around Great Britain.

In 1996 she made her first transatlantic trip (leaving on her 20th birthday).

In 1998 she won (in her class) a solo transatlantic race.

In 1999 she won the Round Europe race 2000.

In 2001 she became the fastest female and youngest sailor to race around the world solo, non-stop – taking 94 days, 4 hours and 25 minutes. She finished second overall.

She was runner-up to David Beckham in the 2001 BBC Sports Personality of the Year.

In 2002 she set a new monohull record in a solo transatlantic race.

In 2004 she missed out on the overall west–east transatlantic record by just 75 minutes.

Time taken to circumnavigate the world (* Denotes Singlehanded)

*2005: Dame Ellen MacArthur – **71 days, 14 hours, 18 minutes and 33 seconds**

*2004: Francis Joyon – **72 days, 22 hours and 54 minutes**

2004: Steve Fossett – **58 days**

2002: Bruno Peyron – **64 days**

1997: Olivier De Kersauson – **71 days**

1994–5: Robin Knox-Johnston/Peter Blake – **74 days**

1993–4: Bruno Peyron – **79 days**

*1989–90: Titouan Lamazou – **109 days**

*1985–6: Dodge Morgan – **150 days**

1983–4: John Ridgway – **193 days** (**two-handed**)

*1970–71: Chay Blyth – **293 days**

*1968–9: Robin Knox-Johnston – **313 days**.
This was the first non-stop solo circumnavigation.
Knox-Johnston was the only sailor – of the 11
who set out at the same time as he did – to
make it.

*1966–7: Francis Chichester – **274 days** – stopping
in Sydney for 48 days (this was the first one-stop
solo circumnavigation). He was 65 years old
but was no stranger to record-breaking, having
become (in 1931) the first person to fly solo
across the Tasman Sea.

Note: In 1519 Ferdinand Magellan led a convoy
of five ships around the world. This first
circumnavigation was an attempt to prove that
the coveted Spice Islands were the property of
Spain. One ship made it back to Seville. Magellan
was not on it; he had died in the battle of Mactan
on Cebu Island in the Philippines.

Sardines

Sardines are sensitive fish. When naval battles take place on their shoaling grounds, they don't return for decades afterwards.

Like all oily fish, sardines (especially fresh ones) are good for the brain and the heart. According to a 1987 study of children, eating sardines can improve your memory.

Traditionally fishermen encouraged sardines to rise to the surface of the sea by drumming their feet on the bottom of the boat. The shoals would then be scooped up.

For years sardines were sold in cans with 'keys' that would break as you tried to turn them, leaving razor-sharp edges. This led to cut fingers, oil going everywhere and no sardines for tea. In the past few years they have been sold flat in cans with a ring-pull (like a soft drink) or standing up in a can that is opened with a tin opener (like a can of baked beans).

In Britain, tinned sardines are one of our cheapest foods. If we want to describe someone as broke, we talk about them living on a diet of sardines.

The French take sardines seriously. In southern France there is a museum dedicated to sardines. The museum's creator said, 'The fish are part of our culture.'

In 1994, in Lima, Peru, 1,500 young people made a three-mile-long sardine sandwich in an attempt to get into *The Guinness Book of Records*.

Some countries and their symbols

Russia – **the bear**

China – **the dragon**

Japan – **cherry blossom**

US – **the eagle**

Turkey – **the tulip**

Greece – **the olive branch**

New Zealand – **the kiwi**

Bulgaria – **the lion**

India – **the Bengal tiger**

Denmark – **the beech tree**

Australia – **the kangaroo**

Canada – **the maple leaf**

Scotland – **the thistle**

Christmas

Armenians celebrate Christmas on 19 January.

The *Mayflower* arrived at Plymouth Rock, Massachusetts, on Christmas Day 1620.

The world's first Christmas stamp was issued by Austria in 1937.

The first electric Christmas lights were put together by a telephone switchboard installer.

In about 1597 William Shakespeare gave *The Merry Wives of Windsor* to Queen Elizabeth I for Christmas.

***Rudolph, the Red-Nosed Reindeer* was created in 1939, in Chicago, as a Christmas promotion for the Montgomery Ward department stores. The lyrics were written by Robert May, but weren't set to music until 1947. Gene Autry recorded the hit song in 1949.**

There are three American towns named Santa Claus.

The worst Christmas cracker jokes?

Q. Why do barbers make good drivers?
A. They know the short cuts.

Q. Why do elephants have wrinkled skin?
A. Have you ever tried to iron an elephant?

Q. What do you call a big green thing that sits in the corner and cries?
A. The Incredible Sulk.

Q. Why do birds fly south in winter?
A. It's too far to walk.

Q. When is a girl like a telephone?
A. When she's engaged.

Q. What has eyes but can't see?
A. A potato.

Q. Why does Santa Claus have a garden?
A. He likes to hoe hoe hoe.

Q. What has teeth but never eats?
A. A comb.

Q. Why did the biscuit cry?

A. Because his mum and dad had been a wafer so long.

What people in different countries eat for Christmas dinner

Hungary – Fish soup and fried fish

Romania – Bread-based Christmas cake

Iceland – Smoked lamb

Jamaica – Curried goat, rice and gungo peas

Latvia – Sausage, cabbage and brown peas in a pork sauce

Nicaragua – Chicken stuffed with fruit and vegetables

Ukraine – Meat broth

Denmark – Roast duck

Finland – Turkey casserole with carrots, macaroni, potatoes and swede

Germany – Roast goose

Greenland – Seabirds wrapped in the skin of a seal

Luxembourg – Venison, hare and black pudding

Norway – Cod or haddock and Christmas meatloaf

Brazil – Turkey marinated in rum, and ham, with coloured rice

Czech Republic – Fish soup, salad, carp and eggs

Portugal – Salted cod and potatoes

Russia – Goose and suckling pig

Sweden – Herring, ham and meatballs

Animals

The South American giant anteater eats more than 30,000 ants a day.

Camel milk does not curdle.

A grasshopper needs a minimum air temperature of 16°C before it's able to hop.

Polar-bear liver contains so much vitamin A that it could be fatal to a human if eaten.

The greater dwarf lemur in Madagascar always gives birth to triplets.

Somalia has more goats than people.

Giraffes have no vocal cords.

An anaconda can swallow a pig.

Nearly all polar bears are left-handed.

The only country with a national dog is the Netherlands (the Keeshond).

There are no furry animals native to Antarctica.

A dzo is the offspring of a yak and a cow.

A geep is the offspring of a sheep and a goat.

Pigs can become addicted to alcohol.

Sir Anthony Hopkins (black-footed penguin) and Rolf Harris (koala) both 'adopted' animals at London Zoo.

The average porcupine has more than 30,000 quills. Porcupines are excellent swimmers. Their quills are hollow and act like floating aids.

Skunk litters are born in April.

If a pig is sick, it stops curling its tail.

Camels refuse to carry loads that are not properly balanced.

Female alligators protect their young for up to two years after they have hatched (which is more mothering than most reptiles get).

The Mojave ground squirrel, found mainly in the American West, hibernates for eight months a year.

Llamas are said to be inquisitive and friendly. They softly blow on each other as a way of saying hello. They also make good guards for livestock.

Squirrels might live for 15 or 20 years in captivity, but their lifespan in the wild, where they fall victim to disease, malnutrition, predators, cars and humans, is much shorter.

The individual hair of a chinchilla is so fine that 500 of them equal the thickness of a single human hair.

There are fewer than 1,000 Bactrian camels left in the wild.

Celebrities who were in the National Youth Theatre

Orlando Bloom

Rosamund Pike

Matt Lucas

David Walliams

Sir Ben Kingsley

Dame Helen Mirren

Daniel Craig

Daniel Day-Lewis

Timothy Spall

David Suchet

Liza Tarbuck

Jamie Theakston

Alex Kingston

Plants

The hurricane plant has holes in its leaves which keep it from being destroyed by strong winds.

The word dandelion comes from the French *dent de lion*, meaning 'lion's tooth'.

Hydrangeas produce pink and white flowers in alkaline soil and blue ones in acidic soil.

No wild plant produces a flower or blossom that is absolutely black.

Only two flowering plants grow in Antarctica. One is grass and the other is a relative of the carnation.

Strange names of flowers and plants

Dog's-Tooth Grass

Old Man's Beard

Jack-Go-to-Bed-at-Noon

Witches' Butter

None So Pretty

Morning Glory

Love-in-Idleness

Devil's Snuffbox

Gill-over-the-Ground

Elephant's Ears

People who had flowers named after them

Prince William
(rose)

Madonna
(gladiolus)

Carol Vorderman
(fuchsia – named
'Countdown Carol')

Liv Tyler (rose)

Charlie Dimmock
(fuchsia)

Alan Titchmarsh
(dianthus, lupin
and fuchsia)

**Camilla, Duchess
of Cornwall** (rose)

Katie Melua
(tulip)

Dolphins

Dolphins can jump
6 metres above the
water surface.

**Ganges river dolphins are
virtually blind. All they
can 'see' is the direction
and intensity of light. This
is one of the reasons why
they swim on one side,
with one flipper trailing in
the muddy riverbed.**

In 340BC Aristotle observed
that dolphins gave birth
to live young that were
attached to their mother
by umbilical cords. For
this reason he considered
dolphins and related
creatures to be mammals.
24 centuries later,
biologists agreed with him.

Dolphins can reach speeds of 37 mph (60 kph).

Dolphins swim in circles while they sleep with the eye on the outside of the circle open to keep watch for predators. After a certain amount of time, they reverse and swim in the opposite direction with the opposite eye open.

Some 'lands'

Land of the Free (**US**)

Land of My Fathers (**Wales**)

Land of the Long White Cloud (**New Zealand**)

Land of Enchantment (**Mexico**)

Land of the Rising Sun (**Japan**)

Land of Dance (**Cuba**)

Land of Mystery (**India**)

Land of the People (**China**)

Land of Opportunity (**Canada**)

Land of Hope and Glory (**England**)

Religion

The religion of the Todas people of southern India forbids them to cross any kind of bridge.

Some saints in the Middle Ages were dirty because they thought it would bring them closer to God.

Belief in the existence of vacuums used to be punishable by death under Church law.

There's a temple in Sri Lanka dedicated to a tooth of the Buddha.

In 1654 Bishop Ussher of Ireland, having analysed all the 'begats' in Genesis, concluded that planet Earth had been created at 9 a.m. on 26 October 4004BC, a Thursday.

St John was the only one of the twelve apostles to die a natural death.

Pope Paul IV was so outraged when he saw the naked bodies on the ceiling of the Sistine Chapel that he ordered Michelangelo to paint garments on them.

The term 'devil's advocate' comes from the Roman Catholic Church. When considering whether someone should be created a saint, a devil's advocate was appointed to give an alternative view.

David is the most common name in the Bible. Jesus is second.

The word Sunday is not in the Bible.

The newest states in the USA

Hawaii (joined the Union in August 1959)

Alaska (January 1959)

Arizona (February 1912)

New Mexico (January 1912)

Oklahoma (November 1907)

Utah (January 1896)

Idaho (July 1890)

Wyoming (July 1890)

Montana (November 1889)

Washington (November 1889)

The Simpsons

The Simpsons started out as a short insert on *The Tracey Ullman Show* but soon became a half-hour prime-time show. It is now the longest-running American sitcom as well as the longest-running American animated programme.

Evergreen Terrace, the Simpsons' street, is the name of the street where the show's creator, Matt Groening, grew up in Portland, Oregon.

Many of the characters in the show are named after streets in Portland, Oregon. These include Flanders, Kearney, Lovejoy, Quimby and Terwilliger (Sideshow Bob).

Homer's grunt – D'oh! – has entered the English dictionary.

The doorknocker on the Simpsons' front door looks a lot like Mr Burns – complete with liver spots and pointy nose.

***The Simpsons* is the only sitcom to have had 'appearances' from three former Beatles (Paul, George and Ringo).**

Initially, Yeardley Smith auditioned for the voice of Bart and Nancy Cartwright for the voice of Lisa. They play them the other way around.

Dan Castellaneta, the voice of Homer, based the voice on his own father's voice.

No one knows where Springfield, the Simpsons' home town, is, and the writers often tease the audience. For example, in one episode, Marge phones an egg-painting company and, when asked for her address, says, '742 Evergreen Terrace, Springfield, Ohi–', but continues, 'Oh hiya, Maude!' speaking to the person who has just appeared in her kitchen.

Hank Azaria, the voice for many of the characters, says that most of his voices are just bad celebrity impressions. Moe is Al Pacino while Louie the cop is Sylvester Stallone.

'Appeared' on The Simpsons

Danny DeVito (Herb Powell)

Michelle Pfeiffer (Mindy Simmons)

Sam Neill (Molloy)

Steve Martin (Ray Patterson)

Drew Barrymore (Sophie)

Michael Keaton (Jack)

Pierce Brosnan (Computer)

Ben Stiller (Garth Motherloving)

Reese Witherspoon (Greta Wolfcastle)

Simon Cowell (Henry)

Sarah Michelle Gellar (Gina Vendetti)

Lucy Liu (Madam Wu)

Liam Neeson (Father Sean)

Ricky Gervais (Charles)

Kiefer Sutherland (Jack Bauer)

Most popular breakfasts

France: Croissants, breads, jams, coffee and orange juice.

Germany: Bread rolls with ham, cheese and boiled eggs, and coffee.

Spain: *Chocolate con churros* – batter fried in oil, sprinkled with sugar and dipped in melted chocolate.

The Bahamas: Stewed red snapper with grits.

Barbados: Corn flakes/bran flakes with warm milk, and orange or grapefruit juice.

Israel: Fruit, breads and cheeses.

Poland: Cold meats and breads.

Fiji: Fijian bread and lemongrass tea.

Iceland: Cereal and yoghurt with bread and coffee.

Some British cheeses

Ribblesdale Blue Goat

Black Bevon Welsh

Balcombe Brown Ring

Coquetdale

Kidderton Ash

Lord of the Hundreds

Rothbury Red

Village Green Goat

Coverdale

Blacksticks Blue

Goosnargh Gold

Farmhouse Llanboidy

Fine Fettle Yorkshire

Goldilocks

Black Eyed Susan

Golden Cross

Netting Hill Cheese

Dunsyre Blue

Brinkburn

Innkeepers Choice

Radden Blue

Cotherstone

Bonchester

Katy's White Lavender

Stinking Bishop

Having babies

Some animals and how long they're pregnant for . . .

African elephant
– two years

Rhinoceros
– 18 months

Giraffe – 15 months

Bottlenose dolphin
– one year

Horse – 11 months

Polar bear
– eight months

Cat – nine weeks

Dog – nine weeks

Rabbit – one month

Hamster
– two weeks

Around the world

At any one moment there are about 1,800 thunderstorms taking place on the planet Earth.

Italy's national flag was designed by Napoleon.

If the population of China walked past you in single file, the line would never end because of the rate of reproduction.

No rain has ever been recorded in the Atacama desert in Chile.

The national anthem of Greece is 158 verses long.

7 per cent of the Irish barley crop goes into the making of Guinness.

The only city in the world whose name can be spelled entirely with vowels is Aiea in Hawaii.

Monaco's national orchestra is bigger than its army.

Hurricanes and tornadoes always go clockwise in the southern hemisphere and counterclockwise in the northern hemisphere.

The Zambian authorities don't allow tourists to take pictures of Pygmies.

When flowers are given for romantic reasons in Russia, they're always in odd numbers as an even number of flowers is given at funerals.

The Mexican Hat Dance is the official dance of Mexico.

Brazil borders every country in South America except Chile and Ecuador.

In Turkey the colour of mourning is violet. In most Muslim countries and in China it is white.

The deepest mine in the world is Western Deep Levels near Charletonville, South Africa. It is 2.6 miles (4.2 km) deep.

Peeters is the most common surname in Belgium.

China has more English speakers than the United States.

Mongolians put salt in their tea instead of sugar.

80 per cent of millionaires drive second-hand cars.

Every year there are more births in India than there are people in Australia.

There is a cash machine at McMurdo Station in Antarctica, which has a winter population of 200 people.

India has more post offices than any other country.

People who had airports named after them

John Wayne (Santa Ana)

John F. Kennedy (New York)

Charles de Gaulle (Paris)

Leonardo da Vinci (Rome)

Pope John Paul II (Krakow)

Marco Polo (Venice)

Jomo Kenyatta (Nairobi)

Pablo Picasso (Málaga)

John Lennon (Liverpool)

Chuck Yeager (Charleston)

George Bush (Houston)

Louis Armstrong (New Orleans)

Wolfgang Amadeus Mozart (Salzburg)

George Best (Belfast)

Charles Lindbergh (San Diego)

Ninoy Aquino (Manila)

Benazir Bhutto (Islamabad)

Around the world

The country with the highest density of natural blondes is Finland.

Dutch and Israeli soldiers aren't required to salute officers.

In Italy, the entire town of Capena, just north of Rome, lights up cigarettes each year at the Festival of St Anthony.

It is the custom in Morocco for a bride to keep her eyes closed throughout the marriage ceremony.

The Amayra guides of Bolivia are said to be able to keep pace with a trotting horse for a distance of 62 miles (100 km).

In the Hebrides, what defines an island is the ability of the land to support at least one sheep.

After oil, coffee is the most traded commodity in the world.

Soldiers from every country salute with their right hand.

The Tibetan mountain people use yak milk as a form of currency.

Niagara Falls has moved about 10 miles (7 km) upstream in the last 10,000 years.

Every year in France there is a 'Thieves Fair' where people are encouraged to try to steal things from the stalls.

The Canary Islands were not named after the canary bird. They were named after a breed of large dog. The Latin name was Canariae insulae – 'Island of Dogs'. The bird was named after the islands.

The oldest republic in the world is San Marino, located in Europe. It has been a republic for more than 1,700 years, since 301.

Nine out of ten Canadians live within 100 miles of the US border.

For the Berbers in the Atlas mountains of northern Morocco, the liver, not the heart, is the source of love. When a girl falls in love, she says, 'Darling, you have stolen my liver.'

Hundreds of years ago in Japan, anyone attempting to leave the country was executed.

A Dutch court ruled that a bank robber could deduct the 2,000 euros he paid for his pistol from the 6,600 euros he had to return to the bank he robbed.

There is zero gravity at the centre of the Earth.

The Earth is slowing down – in a few million years there won't be a leap year.

Honey

The honey bee is the only insect that produces food eaten by man.

Honey was once used to treat cuts and burns.

The average bee yields only one-twelfth of a teaspoon of honey in its life.

A honey bee visits 50 to 100 flowers during a collection trip.

Worker bees are all female.

Honey lasts for ever. An explorer who found a 2,000-year-old jar of honey in an Egyptian tomb said it tasted delicious.

The Romans used honey instead of gold to pay their taxes.

The term 'bee line' comes from the route bees take to the flower of their choice – the shortest possible.

Honey was part of Cleopatra's daily beauty ritual.

Astronomy

Buzz Aldrin was the second man to walk on the moon. His mother's maiden name was Moon.

All the planets in our solar system could be placed inside the planet Jupiter.

For every extra kilogram carried on a space flight, 530 kilograms of fuel is needed at lift-off.

Summer on Uranus lasts for 21 years – but so does winter.

All the moons of the solar system are given names from Greek and Roman mythology, except the moons of Uranus, which are named after Shakespearean characters.

Neutron stars are so condensed that a fragment the size of a sugar cube would weigh as much as all the people on Earth put together.

In 1963 baseball pitcher Gaylord Perry remarked, 'They'll put a man on the moon before I hit a home run.' On 20 July 1969, a few hours after Neil Armstrong set foot on the moon, Gaylord Perry hit his first – and only – home run.

It takes 8 minutes 12 seconds for sunlight to reach Earth.

The tail of the Great Comet of 1843 was 205 million miles (330 million km) long. (It will return in 2356.)

During a total solar eclipse the temperature can drop by 6°C.

NB: The Mount of Jupiter and the Girdle of Venus are found on the palm of your hand.

Brains

The brain is the second heaviest organ in the human body. The liver is the heaviest; the lungs and the heart come third and fourth.

The brain uses more than 25 per cent of the oxygen required by the human body.

The brain uses less power than a 100-watt bulb.

Albert Einstein's brain was preserved after his death.

Geena Davis, Carol Vorderman, Jamie Theakston and Carol Smillie are all members of MENSA, the organization for people with high IQs.

Onlys

Bill Clinton sent only two emails during his eight-year presidency. One was to John Glenn, one of the original astronauts who went back into space as an old man; the other was to test the email system.

The only Nobel prizewinner also to win an Oscar is George Bernard Shaw (for Pygmalion).

The only two mammals to lay eggs are the platypus and the echidna.

Only 6 per cent of the autographs in circulation from members of the Beatles are believed to be real.

In Germany there's a flea that lives and breeds only in beer mats.

Only male turkeys gobble; females make a clicking noise.

Maine is the only US state with just one syllable. Maine is also the only US state that borders only one other state.

The German writer Goethe, who died in 1832, could write only if he had an apple rotting in the drawer of his desk.

The British writer Rudyard Kipling, who died in 1936, wrote only in black ink.

The Dutch town of Abcoude is the only town in the world whose name begins with ABC.

Only female mosquitoes bite, and only female mosquitoes buzz.

Only two countries have borders on three oceans – the US and Canada.

Early Greek and Roman physicians believed the only way to grow a good crop of basil was to curse while scattering the seeds.

Snails mate only once in a lifetime.

Some words on friendship

'It's not the people you meet in the world – it's the friendships you make on the way.' (Nicole Kidman)

'Friendship is born at that moment when one person says to another: What! You too? I thought I was the only one.' (C. S. Lewis)

'Love demands infinitely less than friendship.' (George Jean Nathan)

'Rare as is true love, true friendship is rarer.' (Jean de la Fontaine)

'Your friends will know you better in the first minute you meet than your acquaintances will know you in a thousand years.' (Richard Bach)

'I always felt that the great high privilege, relief and comfort of friendship was that one had to explain nothing.' (Katherine Mansfield)

'Friendship should be a responsibility, never an opportunity.' (Unknown)

'Be slow to fall into friendship; but when thou art in, continue firm and constant.' (Socrates)

'Friendship is like money, easier made than kept.' (Samuel Butler)

'Friendship is a sheltering tree.' (Samuel Taylor Coleridge)

'Every man passes his life in the search after friendship.' (Ralph Waldo Emerson)

'A friend to all is a friend to none.' (Aristotle)

Words

Before the year 1000 the word 'she' did not exist in the English language. The word appeared only in the 12th century, about 400 years after English began to take form. 'She' probably derived from 'seo', the Viking word referring to all things feminine.

If you mouth the word 'colourful' to someone, it looks like you are saying, 'I love you'.

There is no Albanian word for headache.

The Hawaiian alphabet has only 12 letters.

'Dreamt' is the only English word that ends in the letters 'mt'.

The following words are rarely used in the singular: trivia (trivium), paparazzi (paparazzo), assizes (assize), auspices (auspice), timpani (timpano), minutiae (minutia), graffiti (graffito), scampi (scampo), scruples (scruple), measles (measle).

The following words are rarely used in the positive: inadvertent (advertent), immaculate

(maculate), inclement (clement), disconsolate (consolate), indelible (delible), feckless (feckful), unfurl (furl), insipid (sipid), unspeakable (speakable), unkempt (kempt), incorrigible (corrigible), implacable (placable), ineffable (effable), innocuous (nocuous), impervious (pervious), expurgated (purgated), impeccable (peccable), inevitable (evitable).

Only two words in the English language end in -gry: hungry and angry.

The longest one-syllable word is **SCREECHED**.

APPEASES, ARRAIGNING, HOTSHOTS, SIGNINGS and **TEAMMATE** all have letters which occur twice and only twice.

The sentence 'He believed Caesar could see people seizing the seas' contains seven different spellings of the 'ee' sound.

Each of these words has a letter that repeats six times: **DEGENERESCENCE** (six Es), **INDIVISIBILITY** (six Is) and **NONANNOUNCEMENT** (six Ns).

WEDLOCK is derived from the old English words

for pledge ('wed') and action ('lac').

The shortest English word that contains the letters A, B, C, D, E, and F is **FEEDBACK**.

The word **FREELANCE** comes from a knight whose lance was free for hire.

The word **SHERIFF** comes from 'shire reeve'. In feudal England, each shire had a reeve who upheld the law for that shire.

The Sanskrit word for 'war' means 'desire for more cows'.

Britain's best attractions (as voted for by children)

1. Alton Towers
2. **Thorpe Park**
3. Cadbury World
4. **Blackpool Pleasure Beach**
5. Madame Tussauds
6. **Chessington World of Adventures**
7. The London Eye
8. **The London Dungeon**
9. Legoland
10. **Drayton Manor**

Britain's best attractions (as voted for by parents)

1. Alton Towers
2. **Legoland**
3. Blackpool Pleasure Beach
4. **Cadbury World**
5. The Eden Project
6. **Chester Zoo**
7. The Science Museum
8. **Woburn Safari Park**
9. Thorpe Park
10. **The London Eye**

The Victoria Cross

The Victoria Cross was first issued on 29 January 1856, in recognition of acts of valour during the Crimean War of 1854–5. It is the highest award for bravery that any British or Commonwealth soldier can receive.

The VC is awarded for 'acts of valour in the face of the enemy'. However, between 1858 and 1881 six were awarded for brave acts 'under circumstances of extreme danger' (rather than 'in the face of the enemy').

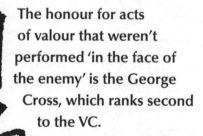

The honour for acts of valour that weren't performed 'in the face of the enemy' is the George Cross, which ranks second to the VC.

Awards of the Victoria Cross are always announced in the pages of the *London Gazette*.

Famously, all VCs are cast from the two bronze cannon that were captured from the Russians at the siege of Sebastopol. However, in his 2006 book, *Bravest of the Brave: The Story of the Victoria Cross*, the historian John Glanfield reveals that this is not true: 'I was astonished,' he has said. 'There was an accepted legend and no one had researched whether it was true. When something has been the belief for 150 years it becomes accepted as the truth.'

A total of 1,355 Victoria Crosses have been awarded since 1856. Three people were awarded the VC twice: Noel Chavasse, Arthur Martin-Leake, both members of the Royal Army Medical Corps, and New Zealander Charles Upham.

Before 1905 the VC couldn't be awarded posthumously. Only one in ten VC recipients in the 20th century is believed to have survived the action for which they received the VC.

Before the 20th century it couldn't be awarded to Indian or African troops. Khudadad Khan became the first Indian soldier to receive one in 1914.

The largest number of VCs awarded on a single day was 24 on 16 November 1857, for the relief of Lucknow.

The largest number of VCs awarded in a single action was 11 at Rorke's Drift on 22 January 1879 (famously recorded in the film *Zulu*).

The largest number of VCs awarded in a single war or conflict was 634 during the First World War.

Since 1945 the VC has been awarded just 12 times. Four were awarded during the Korean War, one in the Indonesia-Malaysia confrontation in 1965, four to Australians in the Vietnam War, two during the Falklands War in 1982, and one in the Second Gulf War in 2005 (to Private Johnson Beharry).

Flying Officer Lloyd Trigg was the only person ever to be awarded a Victoria Cross on evidence provided *solely* by the enemy (during the Second World War). There were no surviving Allied witnesses and the recommendation was made by the captain of the German U-boat sunk by Trigg's aeroplane.

A VC was awarded to the American Unknown Soldier (while the US Medal of Honor was awarded to the British Unknown Warrior).

Jeremy Clarkson's father-in-law won the VC.

VCs are highly prized by collectors and can fetch more than £200,000 at auction. The British businessman and former Conservative Party chairman, Lord Ashcroft, has amassed the largest private collection of about 100 VCs.

The human condition

The human body contains enough iron to make an 8-cm nail.

Girls have more genes than boys, and because of this are better protected from things like colour blindness and haemophilia.

It takes about 200,000 frowns to make a permanent wrinkle.

Intelligent people have more zinc and copper in their hair.

'Phosphenes' are the stars and colours you see when you rub your eyes.

The best way for a boy to know whether he will go bald when he's old is to look at his mother's father.

An average pair of feet sweats half a litre of perspiration a day.

It takes about 150 days for a fingernail to grow from cuticle to fingertip.

The average clean-shaven man will spend five months of his life shaving and will remove 8.5 metres of hair.

The cartilage in the nose never stops growing, which is why you see old men with big noses.

The average adult has a vocabulary of 5,000 to 6,000 words.

You burn 3.5 calories each time you laugh.

The kidneys use more energy than the heart (kidneys use 12 per cent of available oxygen; the heart uses 7 per cent).

Human thighbones are as strong as concrete.

The average lifespan of a taste bud is 10 days

It takes 25 muscles to swallow.

The mouth produces a litre of saliva a day.

The eye is a self-cleaning organ.

While sleeping, one man in eight snores, and one in ten grinds his teeth.

Male patients fall out of hospital beds twice as often as female patients.

A foetus acquires fingerprints in the womb at the age of three months.

The human body has 600 muscles, which make up 40 per cent of the body's weight. We use 300 of these muscles to stand still. We need 72 muscles to speak. If all 600 muscles in your body pulled in one direction, you could lift 25 tons.

Six-year-olds laugh about 300 times a day.
Adults laugh about 15 times a day.

The attachment of the skin to muscles is what causes dimples.

The most common blood type in the world is type O. The rarest, A-H, has been found in fewer than a dozen people since the type was discovered.

Due to gravitational effects, you weigh slightly less when the moon is directly overhead.

Every year about 98 per cent of the atoms in your body are replaced.

The length of all the eyelashes you shed in a lifetime is about 30 metres.

A cough comes out of your mouth at about 62 mph (100 kph).

Alcohol does not kill brain cells, but detaches them. Reattachment requires new nervous tissue, which cannot be produced after about the age of five.

Transplant firsts

First cornea (front layer of the eye) transplant: 1905

First liver transplant: 1963

First pancreas transplant: 1966

First heart transplant: 1967

First heart-liver transplant: 1984

First heart-liver-kidney transplant: 1989

First hand transplant: 1998

First face transplant: 2005

The nation's all-time favourite top 10 children's programmes *

1. *Rainbow*
2. *The Magic Roundabout*
3.= *Mr Benn*
3.= *Play School*
5. *Bagpuss*
6.= *The Clangers*
6.= *The Wombles*
8. *Trumpton*
9.= *Button Moon*
9.= *Camberwick Green*

*According to a 2006 poll by *CBeebies Weekly*

Some April Fools' Day pranks

In 2007 an illusion designer (for magicians) posted on his website images illustrating the corpse of an unknown eight-inch creation – purporting to be the mummified remains of a fairy. He later sold the 'fairy' on eBay for £280.

In 2006 a Norwegian newspaper devoted an entire page to 'raindrop power' – an alternative to oil as a primary energy source. Readers were invited to write to the energy company to receive the power generated for free.

In 2005 a news story was posted on the official NASA website claiming that there was a picture of water on Mars. In fact, it was a picture of a glass of water on a Mars Bar.

In 2005 Peter Jackson, the director of *King Kong*, aided by cast members, crew members and even a studio representative, announced that *King Kong* would be followed by a sequel, *Son of Kong*, which would see Kong's offspring battle Nazis with shoulder-mounted machine guns.

In 2003 a radio station in Chattanooga, Tennessee, announced that rapper Eminem would be doing a free show in a discount store parking lot. Several police were needed to deal with traffic gridlock. The DJs were jailed for creating a public nuisance.

In 2002 an Australian radio station announced that Athens had lost the 2004 Summer Olympics because they couldn't be ready in time and that Sydney would have to host it again.

In 1998 the Channel 4 show *The Big Breakfast* showed video footage of the Millennium Dome on fire.

In 1998 Burger King ran an ad in USA Today saying that people could get a Whopper for left-handed people with condiments designed to drip out on the right-hand side.

In 1987 a Norwegian newspaper announced that 10,000 litres of illegally smuggled wine had been confiscated and that it would be distributed to the people of Bergen at a local department store. 200 people turned up with bottles and buckets.

In 1979 the TV programme *That's Life!* featured an Old English sheepdog that could drive a car.

The only 12 people to have walked on the moon

Neil Armstrong – 20 July 1969

Edwin 'Buzz' Aldrin – 20 July 1969

Pete Conrad – 19–20 November 1969

Alan Bean – 19–20 November 1969

Alan Shepard – 5–6 February 1971

Edgar Mitchell – 5–6 February 1971

David Scott – 31 July–2 August 1971

James Irwin – 31 July–2 August 1971

Charles Duke – 21–23 April 1972

John Young – 21–23 April 1972

Eugene Cernan – 11–14 December 1972

Harrison Schmitt – 11–14 December 1972

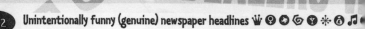

Unintentionally funny (genuine) newspaper headlines

COMPLAINTS ABOUT REFEREES GROWING UGLY

NEW STUDY OF OBESITY LOOKS FOR LARGER TEST GROUP

PUPILS TRAIN AS COUNSELLORS TO HELP UPSET CLASSMATES

DEALERS WILL HEAR CAR TALK AT NOON

TWO SISTERS REUNITE AFTER 18 YEARS AT CHECKOUT COUNTER

WAR DIMS HOPE FOR PEACE

BODY FOUND ON BOAT SEIZED BY BAILIFFS AND DUE TO BE AUCTIONED

TYPHOON RIPS THROUGH CEMETERY; HUNDREDS DEAD

MARCH PLANNED FOR NEXT AUGUST

WOMAN ATTACKED BY TRAIN STATION

BRITON GORED BY BULL IN INTENSIVE CARE

SOMETHING WENT WRONG IN JET CRASH, EXPERT SAYS

COPS QUIZ VICTIM IN FATAL SHOOTING

MOST SURGEONS FACE CUTS

POLICE CHIEF'S PLEDGE TO MURDER WITNESSES

GIANT TEA BAGS PROTEST

INCLUDE YOUR CHILDREN WHEN BAKING COOKIES

CUTS COULD HURT ANIMALS

CHEF THROWS HIS HEART INTO HELPING FEED NEEDY

LESOTHO WOMEN MAKE GREAT CARPETS

GUNMAN SHOT BY 999 COPS

SUBSTITUTE TEACHERS SEEKING RESPECT

NIGHT SCHOOL TO HEAR PEST TALK

MAD COW TALKS

MAN FOUND BEATEN, ROBBED BY POLICE

JUVENILE COURT TO TRY SHOOTING DEFENDANT

SQUAD HELPS DOG BITE VICTIM

THUGS EAT THEN ROB PROPRIETOR

ENRAGED COW INJURES FARMER WITH AXE

GRANDMOTHER OF EIGHT MAKES HOLE IN ONE

DEFENDANT'S SPEECH ENDS IN LONG SENTENCE

HOSPITALS SUED BY SEVEN FOOT DOCTORS

DEADLINE PASSES FOR STRIKING POLICE

SUDDEN RUSH TO HELP PEOPLE OUT OF WORK

ALEXANDER HOPING PAST IS BEHIND HIM

MINERS REFUSE TO WORK AFTER DEATH

HALF OF ALL CHILDREN TESTED SCORED BELOW
AVERAGE

STOLEN PAINTING FOUND BY TREE

KIDS MAKE NUTRITIOUS SNACKS

POLICE SEARCH FOR WITNESSES TO ASSAULT

LAWYERS GIVE POOR FREE LEGAL ADVICE

Very punny! The names of genuine hairdressing salons

Hairport
Fringe Benefits
The Clip Joint
Power Cuts
Hairs & Graces
Millionhairs
Streaks Ahead
Head Office
Snipping Image
A Head of Time
Hairloom
Shear Success
A Cut Above
Curl Up 'n' Dye

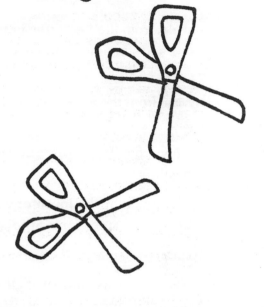

Some explanations of brand names

Harpic: from the first three letters of the first name and surname of the man who developed it – Harry Pickup.

Ryvita: from the word 'rye' and the Latin for life, *vita*.

Findus: from the words 'fruit industries' (i.e. F and Indus).

7-Up: named by the inventor who had already rejected six names for his product.

Mazda: named after the Persian god of light.

Hovis: derives its name from the Latin words *hominis vis*, meaning 'man's strength'.

Lego: from the Danish words *leg godt*, meaning 'play well'.

Things that started in the 1950s

Rock 'n' roll, **X-certificate films**, nuclear submarines, **the Planetarium at Madame Tussauds**, televising of Rugby League matches, **credit cards**, the Mini car, **tea bags**, the Frisbee, **parking meters**, Disneyland, *The Guinness Book of Records*, space travel, **Lego**, ITV (and, therefore, TV commercials), **diet soft drinks** (**no-cal ginger ale**), the Eurovision Song Contest, **Barbie dolls**, comprehensive schools, **fishfingers**, automatic electric kettles, **TV situation comedies (sitcoms)**, yellow no-parking lines, **microwave ovens**, the Velcro fastener, *Blue Peter*, zebra crossings, **Premium Bonds**, *The Mousetrap*, **British motorways**, life peers, **postcodes**, non-stick saucepans, **supermarket chains**, go-karts, **polio vaccines**, roll-on deodorants, **boutiques**, Legal Aid.

Things that started in the 1960s

Jiffy bags, **aluminium kitchen foil**, flavoured potato crisps, **plastic carrier-bags**, trainers, **hatchbacks**, self-service petrol stations, **tights (in the UK)**, fruit-flavoured yoghurts, **After Eight mints**, pocket calculators, *Coronation Street*, fibre-tip pens, **colour TV,** MOT tests on cars, **longlife milk**, the *Sun* newspaper, **electric toothbrushes**, safety belts, **Pedigree Chum**, ASDA, **Green Shield stamps**, James Bond films, **Ibuprofen**, Radio 1, **Songs of Praise**, BBC2, **Mothercare**, Twister, **Mr Kipling**, Pringles, **Fairy Liquid**, clingfilm, **the Jacuzzi**, bar codes on products.

Things that started in the 1970s

The Argos catalogue, ***The Antiques Road Show***, the CD, ***Grange Hill***, *Scoobie Doo*, **Mr Sheen**, Pot Noodle, **soft contact lenses**, floppy disks, **the VCR**, Post-It Notes, **word processors**, North Sea oil, **decimal currency**, VAT, **commercial radio (legal)**, the Cricket World Cup, **test-tube babies**.

Famous people and the foreign languages they can speak

J. K. Rowling (French)

Alex Kingston (German)

Jodie Foster (French)

Rosamund Pike (German and French)

Sophie Raworth (French and German)

Greg Kinnear (Greek)

Orlando Bloom (French)

Condoleezza Rice (Russian)

Gary Lineker (Spanish)

Kylie Minogue (French)

Edward Norton (Japanese)

Mira Sorvino (Mandarin Chinese)

Kate Beckinsale (French and Russian – which she studied at Oxford University)

Ioan Gruffudd (Welsh)

Geena Davis (Swedish)

Davina McCall (French)

Rachel Weisz (German)

Helena Bonham Carter (French)

Rupert Everett (French and Italian)

Sandra Bullock (German)

Salma Hayek (Arabic)

Renée Zellweger (German)

Al Gore (Spanish)

Fiona Bruce (French and Italian)

Lucy Liu (Mandarin Chinese)

Spooky Lincoln–Kennedy coincidences

Abraham Lincoln and John F. Kennedy were both presidents of the USA but they had a lot more in common than just that . . .

Lincoln was elected President in 1860 (having been elected to Congress in 1846); **Kennedy** was elected President in 1960 (having been elected to Congress in 1946).

Both presidents were directly concerned in civil rights for black people.

Lincoln had a secretary named **Kennedy**; **Kennedy** had a secretary named **Lincoln**.

Both presidents were shot in the head (from behind) and both presidents were with their wives when they were assassinated.

Both assassinations took place on a Friday and both presidents were warned that they might be assassinated but both refused to change their schedules.

Lincoln was shot in a theatre by a man who hid in a warehouse; **Kennedy** was shot from a warehouse by a man who hid in a theatre.

Kennedy was riding in a **Lincoln** when he was shot.

Lincoln's assassin (John Wilkes Booth) was a Southerner in his twenties; **Kennedy's** assassin (Lee Harvey Oswald) was a Southerner in his twenties (both assassins were known by their three names).

Booth and Oswald were both shot before they could be tried.

Lincoln was succeeded by his vice-president, Andrew Johnson, who was born in 1808; **Kennedy** was succeeded by his vice-president, Lyndon Johnson, who was born in 1908.

Lincoln and **Kennedy** each had seven letters in their names; John Wilkes Booth and Lee Harvey Oswald each had 15 letters in their names; Andrew Johnson and Lyndon Johnson each had 13 letters in their names.

Slogans seen outside churches

Glory, Glory, Man Utd.

Come in for a faith-lift.

Seven prayer-less days make one spiritually weak.

Come to Church in September and avoid the Christmas rush.

Come to Ch**ch. What is missing? (UR – get it?)

Fight truth decay – brush up your Bible every day.

Is life a Blur? Come to the Oasis.

No God – No Peace. Know God – Know Peace.

Free Trip to Heaven. Details Inside!

When down in the mouth, remember Jonah. He came out all right.

Sign broken. Message inside this Sunday.

How will you spend eternity – Smoking or Non-smoking?

Do not wait for the hearse to take you to church.

If you're headed in the wrong direction, God allows U-turns.

In the dark? Follow the Son.

If you can't sleep, don't count sheep. Talk to the Shepherd.

Celebrities

Amanda Holden likes to do crochet.

Enrique Iglesias is a keen windsurfer.

Jeremy Paxman loves jet-skiing.

Ashton Kutcher has two webbed toes on his left foot.

Neil Diamond once walked around Australia wearing a shirt that said, I'M NOT NEIL DIAMOND. I JUST LOOK LIKE HIM.

Boris Karloff's elaborate make-up for the 1931 horror flick *Frankenstein* was copyrighted.

Elvis Presley wore a cross, a Star of David, and the Hebrew letter *chi*, saying, 'I don't want to miss out on heaven due to a technicality.'

Elvis treated his hair so harshly with dyes and styling products that by the time he was forty it had turned totally white.

When **George Lucas** was mixing the *American Graffiti* soundtrack, he numbered the reels of film with an R and the dialogue with a D. Sound

designer Walter Murch asked George for Reel 2, Dialogue 2 by saying 'R2D2'. George liked the way it sounded so much he used it on another project . . .

Charisma Carpenter is a keen skydiver.

William H. Macy believes that he was a dog – a golden retriever – in a previous life.

Walt Disney's autograph bears no resemblance to the famous Disney logo.

Paul Newman stopped signing autographs 'when I was standing at a urinal and a guy came up with a pen and paper. I wondered: do I wash first and then shake hands?'

AJ McLean has never blown his nose ('When it comes to anything mucus-oriented or phlegm or someone spitting, I gag').

Eddie Murphy crosses himself before he enters lifts.

Lucy Liu practises the martial art of Kali-Eskrima-Silat (knife and stick fighting).

The most densely populated countries

1. **Monaco** (16,620 people per square kilometre)
2. **Singapore** (6,389)
3. **Vatican City** (2,093)
4. **Malta** (1,261)
5. **The Maldives** (1,163)
6. **Bahrain** (1,035)
7. **Bangladesh** (1,002)
8. **Barbados** (647)
9. **Taiwan** (636)
10. **Nauru** (621)
11. **Mauritius** (603)
12. **South Korea** (491)
13. **San Marino** (471)
14. **Tuvalu** (447)
15. **The Netherlands** (395)
16. **Lebanon** (367)
17. **Belgium** (339)
18. **Israel** (338)

19. **Japan** (337)

20. **India** (328)

NB The **UK** is 33rd (243)

The way we live

If you gave each human on Earth an equal portion of dry land, including the uninhabitable areas, everyone would get roughly 30 square metres.

The average smell weighs 760 nanograms.

If we had the same mortality rate now as in 1900, more than half the people alive today would be dead.

If Britain's gas mains were laid end to end, they would go round the world a dozen times.

If all the carpets sold in a year in Britain were laid end to end, they would go all the way to the moon and halfway back again.

55 per cent of women apply lipstick daily.

Lipstick outsells all other cosmetics by four to one.

It's estimated that you will spend one year of your life looking for things you've lost.

Only 1.6 per cent of the water on Earth is fresh.

The calendar repeats itself every 14 years.

Perfume is frequently made from – among other things – a slippery, musky substance called ambergris that is vomited up by certain species of whale.

The distances between cities are actually the distances between city halls. When you see a sign 'Manchester – 60 miles', it means it is 60 miles to the city hall in Manchester.

Soldiers avoid marching in step across some bridges so as not to set up a vibration that could destabilize it.

The USA

California has issued driving licences to six people called Jesus Christ.

50 per cent of all marshmallows consumed in the US have been toasted.

In Vermont there are 10 cows for every person.

The *New Yorker* magazine has more subscribers in California than in New York.

On a clear day you can see five states from the top of the Empire State Building: New York, New Jersey, Connecticut, Massachusetts and Pennsylvania.

The US government keeps its supply of silver at the military academy in West Point.

The murder capital of the US is Gary, Indiana.

A party boat filled with 60 men and women capsized in Texas after it passed a nudist beach and all its passengers rushed to one side to have a look.

There's enough concrete in the Hoover Dam to make a 1.2-metre-wide belt round the equator.

In America there's a lawsuit every 30 seconds.

More turkeys are raised in California than in any other state in the US.

Fried chicken is the most popular meal in American restaurants.

There are more than 100 million dogs and cats in the United States. Americans spend more than

$5.4 billion on their pets each year.

**Death Valley derived its name from the many
gold prospectors who died during the 1849
Gold Rush.**

Nine milligrams of rat droppings are allowed in a
kilogram of wheat.

**The New York City Police Department has a
$3.3 billion annual budget, larger than all but
19 of the world's armies.**

7 per cent of Americans claim they never bathe
at all.

**A woman was chewing what was left of her
chocolate bar when she entered a subway
station in Washington DC.
She was arrested and
handcuffed; eating
is prohibited in
subway stations.**

20 per cent of
Americans think
that the Sun orbits
the Earth.

Famous vegetarians

Jude Law

Amanda Holden

Forest Whitaker

Naomi Watts

Natalie Portman

Shannon Elizabeth

Leonardo DiCaprio

Gwyneth Paltrow

Ozzy Osbourne

Sir Paul McCartney

Stella McCartney

Penelope Cruz

Alan Davies

Avril Lavigne

Josh Hartnett

Nelly

Orlando Bloom

Pink

Famous vegans

Dannii Minogue

Alicia Silverstone

Woody Harrelson

Joaquin Phoenix

Kate Moss

Tobey Maguire

Noah Wyle

André 3000

Anagrams

'To be or not to be: that is the
question; whether 'tis nobler
in the mind to suffer the slings
and arrows of outrageous
fortune'

is an anagram of:

'In one of the Bard's best-
thought-of tragedies, our insistent
hero, Hamlet, queries on two fronts
about how life turns rotten'

Eric Clapton (**NARCOLEPTIC**), Andi
Peters (**PEDESTRIAN**) and Britney Spears
(**PRESBYTERIANS**) all have names that can be
anagramatized into single words.

AH, A RISK – **Shakira**
LOAN SHIN, LADY! – **Lindsay Lohan**
CHOIRS HEALING – **Charlie Higson**
IN POSH TRIAL – **Paris Hilton**
WELL I AM SO THIN – **Lewis Hamilton**

RUN ARMY DAY – **Andy Murray**

LEAVING RIVAL – **Avril Lavigne**

ALL IN YELL – **Lily Allen**

SNAIL COORDINATOR – **Cristiano Ronaldo**

SERVER GRANTED – **Steven Gerrard**

FIERCE LOON – **Eoin Colfer**

WORTH HAZY NOTION – **Anthony Horowitz**

IF A FRIEND CALLED – **Daniel Radcliffe**

CARING, I LEAD – **Daniel Craig**

ECCENTRIC MOUTH, MAN – **Martine McCutcheon**

CHAMELEON SIR – **Michael Rosen**

MANURE PLOT – **Paul Merton**

NOT ARENA KING – **Ronan Keating**

'ONLY JERK!' SCREAM – **Jeremy Clarkson**

HER ILLEGAL CHARM SALE – **Sarah Michelle Gellar**

NO ALIENS, DARLING – **Gillian Anderson**

I WARM BILLIONS – **Robin Williams**

VALUES SLIM WIN – **Venus Williams**

ANORAK'S IN TOWN – **Rowan Atkinson**

CAP STAR TREK WIT – **Patrick Stewart**

BEST PG – NEVER LIES – **Steven Spielberg**

GIRLIE LAW HELL – **Geri Halliwell**

BLOB RECREATION – **Robbie Coltrane**

COOL OGRE IMMINENT – **Colin Montgomerie**

BORN INSANE? NO! – **Anne Robinson**

JUST A BROILER – **Julia Roberts**

NO REAL CHARM BENEATH – **Helena Bonham Carter**

RUDE? I'M HYPED! – **Eddie Murphy**

Science and nature

The Sun is only one of 120 million stars in our galaxy.

Hot water is heavier than cold.

The centre of the Earth has a liquid core as hot as the Sun's surface.

The bark of the redwood tree is fireproof. Fires in redwood forests take place inside the trees.

Nutmeg is poisonous if injected.

The poison arrow frog contains enough poison to kill 2,200 people.

A rainbow can occur only when the Sun is 40 degrees or less above the horizon.

In ten minutes, a hurricane releases more energy than all the world's nuclear weapons combined.

Magnesium was used in early flash photography because it burns with a brilliant light.

A scientific satellite needs only 250 watts of power to operate.

The letter J does not appear on the periodic table of the elements.

Minus 40° Celsius is exactly the same temperature as minus 40° Fahrenheit.

Radio waves travel so much faster than sound waves that a broadcast voice can be heard sooner 11,200 miles (18,000 km) away than at the back of the room in which it originated.

In an atom, the electron weighs 1/2000th the weight of the proton.

When scientists at Australia's Parkes Observatory began picking up radio waves, they thought they had proof of alien life. However, it transpired that the emissions came from a microwave oven in the building.

Hydrogen gas is the least dense substance.

Ocean waves can travel as fast as a jet plane.

Aspirin was the first drug offered as a water-soluble tablet, in 1900.

Copper exposed to arsenic turns black.

A whip 'cracks' because its tip moves faster than the speed of sound.

Water freezes faster if it starts from a warm temperature than a cool one.

Sound travels 15 times faster through steel than through air.

It is harder to reach the speed of sound at sea level than at altitude.

Every megabyte sent over the Internet would need two lumps of coal to power it.

A car travelling at 50 mph (80 kph) needs half its fuel just to overcome wind resistance.

Pure trivia

The flashing warning light on the cylindrical Capitol Records tower spells out HOLLYWOOD in Morse code.

The only one of his sculptures Michelangelo signed was the *Pietà*, completed in 1500.

Linoleum (lino), the floor covering used in many kitchens, was patented in 1863 by Frederick Walton of London.

The typewriter was patented by Henry Mill in 1714, but he never managed to market his invention.

The largest number of horses assembled for a film was 8,000 for King Vidor's epic *War and Peace* (1956).

Paper was invented early in the 2nd century by the Chinese.

The name 'Yucatan' comes from the Maya for 'listen to how they speak' – which is what the Maya said when they first heard the Spanish.

The first colour photograph was made in 1861 by James Maxwell. He photographed a tartan ribbon.

Carbonated soda water was invented in 1767 by Joseph Priestley, the discoverer of oxygen.

Dry cleaning was invented in 1849 by a Monsieur Jolly-Bellin of France, who discovered the process by mistake when he upset a lamp over a newly laundered tablecloth and found that the part that was covered with spirit from the lamp was cleaner than the rest.

Naturalists use marshmallows to lure alligators out of swamps.

The problem of missing teeth was first discussed at length in 1728 by Pierre Fauchard in his book The Surgeon Dentist.

The biro, invented by Hungarian refugee Laszlo Bíró, was first used by the US air force in the Second World. On 9 October 1945 it was put on sale to the public in a New York department store. Over 5,000 people crammed in to buy biros at the costly sum of $12.50 each. Full-page ads promised people the pen would work equally well at altitude and at ground level, underwater and on dry land.

Cream weighs less than milk.

A snail has two pairs of tentacles on its head. One pair is longer than the other and houses the eyes. The shorter pair is used for smelling and feeling its way around.

The artist Picasso could draw before he could walk and his first word was the Spanish word for pencil.

The shortest stage play is Samuel Beckett's *Breath* – 35 seconds of screams and heavy breathing.

The 17th-century French Cardinal Mazarin never travelled without his personal chocolate-maker.

In 1973 a Swedish confectionery salesman named Roland Ohisson was buried in a coffin made of chocolate.

82 per cent of the workers building the Panama Canal – which opened in 1914 – suffered from malaria.

The Romans used porcupine quills as toothpicks.

Extraordinary executions and non-executions

In the 18th and 19th centuries people – including children – were hanged for trivial offences. In 1819 **Thomas Wildish** was hanged for letter-stealing; in 1750 **Benjamin Beckonfield** was hanged for stealing a hat; in 1833 an unnamed nine-year-old boy was hanged for stealing a pennyworth of paint from a shop; in 1782 a 14-year-old girl was hanged for being found in the company of gypsies.

In 1948 William John Gray **was sentenced to hang for the murder of his wife. However, he was reprieved after medical examiners ruled that hanging would cause him too much pain. (He had an injured jaw, which was deemed too weak to hold the rope round his neck.)**

In 1679 **Messrs Green**, **Berry** and **Hill** were hanged at Tyburn for a murder they committed on . . . Greenberry Hill.

On 16 August 1264, at precisely nine o'clock in the morning, Inetta de Balsham **was hanged. The King's messenger arrived a few seconds later with a reprieve. The hangman ran up the stairs and cut the rope with a sword. The victim's face had turned blue but she survived.**

Similarly, in 1705 **John Smith** was hanged for burglary at Tyburn. After he had been hanging for 15 minutes, a reprieve arrived and he was cut down. He was revived and managed to recover. He became known as John 'Half-Hanged' Smith.

In 1736 Thomas Reynolds **was hanged for robbery at Tyburn. He was cut down and placed in a coffin. However, as the hangman's assistant was putting on the lid, it was pushed away and the assistant's arm was grabbed from within. Reynolds was taken out of the coffin and to a nearby house, where he vomited three pints of blood and died.**

In 1650, charged with the murder of her newborn baby (a crime that only ceased to be a capital offence in 1922), **Anne Green** was hanged at Oxford Gaol. After an hour, she was cut down but was seen to be twitching. Her body was passed on to a professor of anatomy, who was preparing to cut her open when he heard a noise from her throat. She was put into a warm bed and her breathing restarted. By the next day she was fully recovered. She was eventually pardoned.

On 23 February 1885 John Lee **was due to be hanged at Exeter Gaol for the murder of his employer (on thin evidence). However, after the hangman put the noose round his neck, the scaffold's drop wouldn't respond to the lever. Lee was returned to his cell while the hangman tested the drop until it worked perfectly. A second attempt was made but, once again, the drop didn't work. When Lee stood on the scaffold for the third time, it again proved impossible. Lee was returned to his cell and later given a reprieve by the Home Secretary. He became famous as 'The Man They Couldn't Hang'.**

Being a hangman was no insurance against being hanged. Four English hangmen were hanged: **Cratwell** in 1538 for robbing a booth at St Bartholomew's Fair; **Stump-leg** in 1558 for thieving; **Pascha Rose** in 1686 for housebreaking and theft; and **John Price** in 1718 for murder.

Postscript: Albert Pierrepoint **was Britain's last executioner. He hanged more than 400 people. After his retirement he campaigned for abolition, saying, 'I do not now believe that any of the hundreds of executions I carried out has in any way acted as a deterrent against future murder. Capital punishment, in my view, achieved nothing except revenge.'**

History

When Leonardo da Vinci's *Mona Lisa* was stolen from the Louvre in 1912, six replicas were sold as the original, each at a huge price, in the three years before the original was recovered.

Dante died on the very day in 1321 that he finished writing his masterpiece, *The Divine Comedy*.

When the sculptor Auguste Rodin exhibited his first major work, *The Bronze Period*, in 1878, it was so realistic that people thought he had sacrificed a live model inside the cast.

Rodin died of frostbite in 1917 when the French government refused him financial aid for a flat, yet they kept his statues warmly housed in museums.

In 1816 J. R. Ronden tried to stage a play that didn't contain the letter 'a'. The Paris audience was offended, rioted and refused to allow the play to finish.

Painter Paul Gauguin was a labourer on the Panama Canal.

Japan did not send an ambassador to another nation until 1860.

In 16th-century Turkey, drinking coffee was punishable by death.

Huge stone wheels were once used as currency by the Yap Islanders of Micronesia.

In the Middle Ages, the highest court in France ordered the execution of a cow for injuring someone.

Charles Dickens earned as much for his lectures as he did for his 20 novels.

In medieval Japan it was fashionable for women to have black teeth.

When the pilgrim ship the *Mayflower* was no longer needed, it was taken apart and rebuilt as a barn.

Russia's Peter the Great taxed men who wore beards.

In the 19th century, in an attempt the debunk the myth that Friday was an unlucky day for mariners, the British navy named a new ship HMS *Friday*,

found a Captain Friday to command it and sent it to sea on a Friday. Neither ship nor crew were heard of again.

In 18th-century English gambling dens, there was an employee whose only job was to swallow the dice in the event of a police raid.

The streets of ancient Mesopotamia were knee-deep in rubbish, since there was no effective way of getting rid of it.

Famous people who were adopted

Nicole Richie

Roman Abramovich

K. T. Tunstall

Andy McNab

Eric Clapton

Dame Kiri Te Kanawa

Anna Ryder Richardson

John Thomson

Ray Liotta

Nicky Campbell

More wisdom of Mark Twain
(see *How To Avoid a Wombat's Bum*)

'There are several good protections against temptation, but the surest is cowardice.'

'Always do right. This will gratify some people, and astonish the rest.'

'When angry, count to four; when very angry, swear.'

'A flea can be taught everything a Congressman can.'

'It takes your enemy and your friend – working together – to hurt you to the heart: the one to slander you and the other to get the news to you.'

'Man: a creature made at the end of the week's work when God was tired.'

'Confession may be good for my soul, but it sure plays hell with my reputation.'

'The public is the only critic whose opinion is worth anything at all.'

'Such is the human race, often it seems a pity that Noah didn't miss the boat.'

'Good breeding exists in concealing how much we think of ourselves and how little we think of the other person.'

Famous people with famous ancestors

Mike Myers – William Wordsworth (poet)
Cate Blanchett – Louis Blériot (inventor and pilot)
Tom Hanks – Abraham Lincoln (US president)
Helena Bonham Carter – Herbert Asquith (British prime minister)
Queen Sofia of Spain – Queen Victoria
Sophie Dahl – Roald Dahl (author)
Gena Lee Nolin – Sir Isaac Newton (scientist)
Al Murray – William Makepeace Thackeray (writer)
Jodie Kidd – Lord Beaverbrook (newspaper proprietor)
Adam Hart-Davis – King William IV
Wayne Rooney – Bob Fitzsimmons (world champion boxer)

Celebrities and what they collect

Rod Stewart – Hornby trainsets

Brian May – old photographs

Dame Judi Dench – dolls' houses and furniture

Vic Reeves – bird and animal skulls

Tom Hanks – 1940s typewriters

Brendan Fraser – vintage Polaroid cameras

Nicolas Cage – antique watches

Lenny Henry – American comic books

Brad Pitt – chairs

Marilyn Manson – vintage metal lunchboxes

Penelope Cruz – coat hangers (she has over 500)

Patrick Stewart – *Beavis and Butthead* merchandise

Helena Christensen – perfume bottles

Pink – stuffed frogs

Tara Palmer-Tomkinson – DO NOT DISTURB signs from hotels around the world

George W. Bush – autographed baseballs

Bill Clinton – saxophones (real ones and miniatures)

Mike Myers – model soldiers

Philippa Forrester – first-edition children's books

Sarah Michelle Gellar – rare books

Anna Kournikova – dolls from the countries she visits

Peter Jackson – models of Second World War aeroplanes

Prince Charles – loo seats

Famous parents of twins

Sean 'P Diddy' Combs

Dougray Scott

Julia Roberts

Gabby Logan

John Hannah

Vic Reeves

John Terry

Marcia Gay Harden

Jeremy Paxman

Robert De Niro

Fern Britton

Baroness Margaret Thatcher

Mel Gibson

Judy Finnigan

Ben Elton

Gordon Ramsay

George W. Bush

Denzel Washington

Al Pacino

Ally McCoist

Famous people who came from large families

Sol Campbell (one of 10 children)

Mel Gibson (one of 11 children)

Lewis Carroll (one of 11 children)

Ms Dynamite (one of 11 children)

Celine Dion (one of 14 children)

Famous people who overcame stammers

Bruce Willis

Sir Winston Churchill

King George VI

Sam Neill

Charles Darwin

Lewis Carroll

Gareth Gates

Samuel L. Jackson

In the latter part of the 18th century, Prussian surgeons treated stutterers by snipping off portions of their tongues.

Sea life

The quahog, a marine clam, can live for up to 200 years, making it the longest-living ocean creature in the world. Second place goes to the killer whale at 90 years, third is the blue whale at 80 years, fourth is the sea turtle at 50 years and fifth is the tiger shark at 40 years.

Pea crabs (the size of a pea) are the smallest crabs in the world.

Scientists still know very little about the giant squid, except what can be gleaned from the carcasses of about 100 beached squid dating back to 1639. Despite centuries of myths and exciting tales of sightings, more is known about dinosaurs than giant squids.

Schools of South American (Pacific) Humboldt squid have been known to strip 225-kilo marlins to the bone.

Oysters can change sex.

85 per cent of all life on Earth is plankton.

Plankton produce nearly three-quarters of the Earth's oxygen.

At the end of a lobster's second year, it will have grown to only about 5 cm long – still smaller than a jumbo shrimp.

The lethal 'lion's mane' is the world's biggest jellyfish. The largest specimen ever found had a bell of 2.3 metres in diameter, and tentacles longer than a blue whale.

Mussels can thrive in polluted water because of their ability to purify bacteria, fungi and viruses.

During low tides, fiddler crabs darken in colour and emerge from their burrows; during high tides they turn pale and retreat. Kept in a laboratory far away from the ocean, they still keep time with the tide, changing colour as it ebbs and flows.

Only 1 in 1,000 creatures born in the sea survives to maturity.

A sea squirt found in the seas near Japan eats its own brain. When it reaches maturity, it attaches itself to a rock and, with no further need to move, dispenses with its brain by digesting it.

Average number of eggs laid by the female American oyster per year: 500 million. About one oyster will reach maturity.

A red sponge can be broken into a thousand pieces and still reconstitute itself.

In the Caribbean there are oysters that can climb trees.

Men III

These American men can use the Roman numeral III after their names:

Ted Danson

Alec Baldwin

Bill Gates

Eminem (real name Marshall Mathers III)

50 Cent (real name Curtis James Jackson III)

Dinosaurs

The first dinosaur appeared around 225 or 230 million years ago. It was called the Staurikosaurus and it survived for about 5 million years.

The first dinosaur to be given a name was the Iguanodon, found in Sussex in 1823. It was not the first dinosaur to be found.

Dinosaurs didn't eat grass: it didn't exist then.

Dinosaurs lived on Earth for more than 150 million years. That's about 75 times longer than humans have lived on Earth.

Some dinosaurs had tails 12 or 13 metres long.

The dinosaur noises in Jurassic Park came from elephants, geese and slowed-down horses.

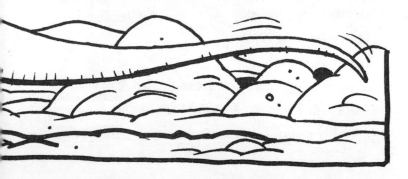

Unusual names famous people have given their children

Princess Tiaamii – Jordan & Peter Andre

D'Lila Star – Sean 'P Diddy' Combs

Deacon – Reese Witherspoon & Ryan Phillippe

Apple – Gwyneth Paltrow & Chris Martin

Salome – Alex Kingston

Emerson Rose – Teri Hatcher

Roan & Laird – Sharon Stone

Kal-el (Superman's name) – Nicolas Cage

Bluebell Madonna – Geri Halliwell

Dusti Rain and KeeLee Breeze – Vanilla Ice

Marquise – 50 Cent

Moon Unit, Dweezil and Diva – Frank Zappa

Dandelion (now Angela) – Keith Richards

Rain – Richard Pryor

Dog – Sky Saxon

Rumer Glenn, Scout Larue and Tallulah Belle – Bruce Willis & Demi Moore

Brooklyn (girl) – Donna Summer

Brooklyn (boy) – Victoria & David Beckham

Missy – Damon Albarn

Piper Maru – Gillian Anderson

Memphis Eve & Elijah Bob Patricius Guggi

Q – Bono

Jesse James Louis – Jon Bon Jovi

Zowie (now Joey) – David Bowie

Phoenix Chi – Mel B

JC – Jackie Chan

Four sons named George – George Foreman

Morgana – Morgan Freeman

Jett – John Travolta

Arrana & Blue Angel – The Edge

Lily-Rose Melody – Johnny Depp & Vanessa Paradis

Gulliver – Gary Oldman

Sage Moonblood & Sistine Rose – Sylvester Stallone

True, Ocean & Sonnet – Forest Whitaker

Arpad Flynn & Aurelius Cy – Elle Macpherson

Lourdes – Madonna

Lennon – Liam Gallagher & Patsy Kensit

Pixie, Fifi Trixiebelle & Peaches – Bob
Geldof
Happy – Macy Gray
Paris – Michael Jackson
Paris – Pierce Brosnan
Eja – Shania Twain
Jermajesty – Jermaine Jackson
Ace – Natalie Appleton & Liam Howlett
Geronimo – Alex James

Geography

There are 1,040 islands around Britain, one of which is the smallest island in the world: Bishop's Rock.

The coastline of Alaska is longer than the entire coastline of the rest of the US (excluding Hawaii).

Seoul, the South Korean capital, means 'the capital' in the Korean language.

The name of Spain comes from 'the land of rabbits'.

In the Andes, time is sometimes measured by how long it takes to smoke a cigarette.

The Sahara desert expands by about 0.6 miles (1 km) a month.

More than 90 per cent of all fish caught are caught in the northern hemisphere.

The smallest island with country status is Pitcairn in Polynesia.

The average North Korean seven-year-old is 7.5 cm shorter than the average South Korean seven-year-old.

The oldest living thing in the world is a creosote bush in south-western California, which is more than 11,000 years old.

The Gulf Stream would carry a message in a bottle at an average of 4 mph (6.5 kph).

The University of Alaska covers four time zones.

500 million years ago, Antarctica was on the equator.

Sahara means 'desert' in Arabic.

Five countries in Europe touch only one other: Portugal, Denmark, San Marino, Vatican City and Monaco.

The American national anthem doesn't mention the name of the country; neither does the Dutch one. In fact, you have to find an ancient and no-longer-sung verse of 'God Save the Queen' to find any mention of Britain.

The Swiss flag is square.

2,000 pounds of space dust and other debris lands on Earth every day.

Coca-Cola is Africa's largest private-sector employer.

Music

Johnny Depp played guitar on 'Fade In-Out' by Oasis.

82 per cent of the Beatles' music was about love.

Kate Moss was namechecked by Lily Allen in the song 'Everything's Just Wonderful', by Jewel in the song 'Intuition' and by Kanye West in the song 'Stronger'.

Irving Berlin, who wrote the song 'White Christmas', never learned to read music or to write it. He hummed or sang his songs to a secretary, who wrote them down in musical notation.

The Beatles' song 'A Day in the Life' ends with a note sustained for 40 seconds.

There are 256 semihemidemisemiquavers in a breve.

Myleene Klass, who among her other talents is a pianist, insured her hands for £1 million.

In 2006 Katie Melua entered *The Guinness Book of Records* for playing the deepest underwater concert (303 metres below sea level on Statoil's Troll A platform in the North Sea).

The term 'rhythm & blues' – later shortened to R&B – was coined in 1948 by Jerry Wexler, to replace the negative term 'Race Records'.

Aerosmith went berserk on their first Japanese tour. On the opening night they destroyed the backstage area when they found turkey roll on the buffet table. Lead singer Steven Tyler commented, 'I explicitly said, "No turkey roll."'

People who play/played in bands

Martine McCutcheon was the lead singer of a three-girl group named **Milan**.

John Simm plays guitar in a band named **Magic Alex**.

Tony Blair was the lead singer in the Oxford University band, the **Ugly Rumours**.

Jamie Oliver played drums in a band named **Scarlet Division**.

Roger Black played bass guitar for the amateur punk group the **Psychedelic Vegetables**.

Russell Crowe is in a band named **30 Odd Foot of Grunts**.

Kevin Bacon formed the **Bacon Brothers** with his older brother Michael (Emmy-winning composer).

Billy Bob Thornton played drums in **Tres Hombres**, a ZZ Top covers band.

Johnny Depp was in a series of garage bands – one of which (**The Kids**) opened for **Iggy Pop**. He is now a member of the band **P** (with **Steve Jones** of the **Sex Pistols** and **Flea** of the **Red Hot Chili Peppers**, among others).

Fiona Bruce was the singer with **Chez Nous**.

Charlie Higson was the lead singer of the band **The Higsons**.

Bruce Willis was in the band **Loose Goose**.

Stephen King and **Matt Groening** are in a band called **Rock Bottom Remainders**.

Instruments and the famous people who can play them

PIANO: Sir Anthony Hopkins, Clint Eastwood, Richard Gere, Rupert Everett, Courteney Cox, Elijah Wood, Pope Benedict XVI, Hugh Jackman, Sean Bean

GUITAR: Serena Williams, Minnie Driver, Kate Hudson, Ricky Gervais, Paul Bettany, Paris Hilton, Tony Blair

SAXOPHONE: James Gandolfini, Darius Danesh, Don Cheadle

CELLO: Prince Charles, Emily Watson, Nicole Richie

TUBA: John Malkovich

ACCORDION: Gabriel Byrne

BASS GUITAR: Daniel Radcliffe (taught by film star Gary Oldman)

MANDOLIN: Nicolas Cage

FRENCH HORN: Ewan McGregor, Samuel L. Jackson

VIOLIN: Russell Crowe

BANJO: Steve Martin, Ewan McGregor

TRUMPET: Samuel L. Jackson, James Gandolfini

TROMBONE: Fiona Phillips

BAGPIPES: Alastair Campbell, Ken Stott

More things Britain gave to the world (see *How To Avoid a Wombat's Bum*)

The mariner's compass, **the pressure cooker**, the match, **the kitchen range**, the machine gun, **gas lighting**, clothes washer and dryer, **the locomotive**, photographic lens, **the**

electromagnet, modern rainwear, **the computer**, photography (on paper), **the pneumatic tyre**, the glider, **linoleum**, colour photography, **the electric vacuum cleaner**, car disc brakes, **the Geiger counter**, stainless steel, **the tank**, the decompression chamber, **the integrated circuit**, genetic fingerprinting, **garden cities**, the hearse, **Christmas cards**

Things invented by Americans

The lightning rod, **bifocals**, the revolver, **the telegraph**, fibreglass, ether as an anaesthetic, the sewing machine, **the safety pin**, the lift, **the oil well**, the typewriter, **the vacuum cleaner**, barbed wire, **denim jeans**, the telephone, **the mechanical cash register**, the light bulb, **the fountain pen**, Coca-Cola, **the hand-held camera**, the automatic telephone exchange, **the juke box**, the zip, **films**, the escalator, **the tractor**, the safety razor, **the electric washing machine**, the electric toaster, **air conditioning**, aircraft autopilot, **the moving assembly line**, the bulldozer, **frozen food**, the car radio, **the personal computer**, the microwave oven, **the video recorder**, the measles vaccine, **the laser**, the CD, **email**

Things invented by the French

The suit, **the tie (based on a style worn in Croatia)**, aluminium ware, **aspirin**, the coffee pot, **the handkerchief**, the Christmas cracker, **the sewing machine**, Teflon utensils, **wallpaper**

Things invented by the Italians

The parachute, **the camera obscura**, the piano, **the pretzel**, the radio, **the espresso machine**, spectacles, **the mariner compass**, the thermometer, **the barometer**, magnets, **the telescope**, scissors, **the mechanical calculator**, the pedometer, **the wind vane**, Fibonacci numbers, **natural plastic**, the ice-cream cone

What some celebrities' fathers do/did for a living

Sienna Miller – Banker

Justin Timberlake – Choir director at a Baptist church

Lewis Hamilton – IT consultant

Russell Crowe – Hotel manager

Paul Merton – Train driver

Daniel Craig – Midshipman in the merchant navy

Brendan Fraser – Tourism executive

Alastair Campbell – Vet

Hugh Grant – Carpet salesman

Damon Albarn – Art school lecturer

Nicky Campbell – Map publisher

Ricky Gervais – Building labourer

Dan Brown – Maths professor

Andrew 'Freddie' Flintoff – Plumber

Les Dennis – Footballer

Nicolas Sarkozy – Advertising agency boss

What some celebrities' mothers do/did for a living

Catherine Tate – Florist

Natasha Kaplinsky – Professor of economics

Lily Allen – Film producer

Anne Hathaway – Lawyer

Lindsay Lohan – Investment banker

David Walliams – Laboratory technician

Russell Brand – Secretary

Coleen McLoughlin – Nursery nurse

Wayne Rooney – Part-time cleaner at the school Coleen McLoughlin attended

Jake Gyllenhaal – Screenwriter

Christian Bale – Circus dancer

Sandra Bullock – Opera singer

Vin Diesel – Psychologist

Kirsten Dunst – Art gallery owner

Colin Firth – Open University lecturer

Alicia Silverstone – Airline stewardess

Laura Linney – Nurse

Tobey Maguire – Secretary

Kylie Minogue – Ballerina

Condoleezza Rice – Pianist

Uma Thurman – Model

Denzel Washington – Beautician

Matt Lucas – Synagogue worker

Celebrities whose mothers or fathers were teachers

Steve Coogan
Michael Rosen
Orlando Bloom
Rhys Ifans
Ben Affleck
David Mitchell
Kevin Bacon
Aled Jones
Dervla Kirwan
Rik Mayall
Amanda Burton
Noel Edmonds
Ioan Gruffudd
Dan Brown

Parents

Uma Thurman's father was the first American to be ordained a Buddhist monk. He taught Tibetan philosophy and civilization at university. Two of his students were Jake and Maggie Gyllenhaal.

Laura Dern was bullied at school because her father – Bruce Dern – was 'the only person to kill John Wayne in the movies'.

Rachel Weisz's father invented the artificial respirator.

Katie Holmes's father, Martin, is 6 feet 6 inches tall.

Norman Cook's father was responsible for introducing the bottle bank to Britain.

The fathers of **Gordon Brown**, **John Motson** and **David Tennant** were all clergymen.

Vic Reeves's father and grandfather share his birthday – and his real name of Jim Moir.

The fathers of **Lisa Kudrow**, **Reese**

Witherspoon, **Roger Black**, **Dame Judi Dench**, **Professor Stephen Hawking** and **Hillary Clinton** were all doctors.

The fathers of **Mick Jagger** and **Ewan McGregor** were both PE teachers.

50 Cent, **Prince Michael of Kent** and **Kirsty Young** never knew their fathers.

Alicia Silverstone filed for emancipation from her parents at the age of 15 so that she could work as an adult.

Sean 'P Diddy' Combs's father was murdered when Sean was two.

Naomi Watts's father was Pink Floyd's sound engineer (and Naomi's mobile phone has their song 'Money' as its ringtone).

Al Green's father fed him his pet goat Billy for dinner.

Steve Coogan's father was Peter Kay's school metalwork teacher.

Richard Blackwood's father used to be married to Naomi Campbell's mother.

The fathers of **Sarah Lancashire** and **Victoria Wood** were both writers who wrote episodes of *Coronation Street*.

The fathers of **Russell Crowe** and **Patricia Hodge** were both hoteliers.

The fathers of **Bruce Oldfield**, **Wayne Rooney**, **Rudy Giuliani**, **Frank Sinatra**, **Andre Agassi** and **Paul Weller** were all boxers.

Rufus Sewell's father was an animator who worked on *Yellow Submarine*.

Eric Clapton and **Jack Nicholson** had mothers who the rest of the world thought were their sisters.

50 Cent's mother was only 15 when she gave birth to him.

Charlton Heston's mother's maiden name was Charlton.

Beyoncé's mother's maiden name was Beyincé.

Jarvis Cocker's mother made him wear lederhosen at school, which caused the other children to laugh at him.

The mothers of **Joanne Harris**, **Davina McCall** and **Jodie Foster** are all French.

The mothers of **Eric Bana** and **Leonardo DiCaprio** are both German.

Telly Savalas and **Tommy Lee** both had mothers who won the Miss Greece beauty contest.

Priscilla Presley became a mother again after becoming a grandmother.

Money

In 1987 American Airlines saved $40,000 by eliminating one olive from each salad served in first class.

Throughout the world more Monopoly money is printed in a year than real money.

Woodpecker scalps, porpoise teeth and giraffe tails have all been used as money.

In Monopoly, the most money you can lose in one trip round the board (going to jail only once) is £26,040. The most money you can lose in one turn is £5,070. If, on the other hand, no one ever buys anything, players could eventually break the bank.

The dollar symbol ($) is a U combined with an S.

The largest ocean liners pay a $250,000 toll for each trip through the Panama Canal. The canal generates one third of Panama's entire economy.

Walter Hunt owed a friend $15, which was a large amount of money in 1849. The friend offered to cancel the debt in return for an item made by Walter from a piece of wire. Walter had invented the first safety pin, and it made his friend a millionaire.

Market research has found that light purple makes customers feel like spending money.

After their Civil War, the US sued Great Britain for damages caused by ships the British had built for the Confederacy. The US asked for $1 billion, but settled for $25 million.

Things that money can't buy

The affection of a dog (they either love you or they don't – irrespective of how wealthy you are).

A swan (all swans are owned by the Queen).

A wild donkey (no such animal now exists).

An entry in *Who's Who*.

Membership of the MCC or Glyndebourne (there are long waiting lists that you can't leapfrog no matter how rich you are).

An Aztec bar (Cadbury's don't make them any more).

A full driving licence.

The *Mona Lisa* (like all paintings kept in museums, it's simply not for sale).

A cure for a cold.

A new Citroën 2CV car.

'Rude' number plates (the DVLA won't let anyone have them).

A place at a British university.

A private beach in mainland England (you can buy a private road giving you private access to the shore but you can't buy the beach itself).

Immunity from the law.

A Cuban Red Macaw (the last one disappeared in 1894).

A ticket for a PanAm flight (at least not since 3 December 1991).

A planet (there's an international agreement that prohibits any country or individual from buying one).

A Nobel prize.

Some of Beatrix Potter's characters

Peter Rabbit

Squirrel Nutkin

Benjamin Bunny

Mrs Tiggy-Winkle

Mr Jeremy Fisher

Miss Moppet

Tom Kitten

Jemima Puddle-Duck

Samuel Whiskers

The Flopsy Bunnies

Ginger and Pickles

Mrs Tittlemouse

Timmy Tiptoes

Mr Tod

Pigling Bland

Johnny Town-Mouse

Little Pig Robinson

Names Walt Disney considered and rejected for Snow White's dwarfs

Gloomy, Wheezy, **Shirty**, Sniffy, **Woeful**, Weepy, **Lazy**, Snoopy, **Puffy**, Shorty, **Baldy**, Biggo-Ego, **Burpy**, Gabby, **Jumpy**, Nifty, **Stubby**, Stuffy

When manufacturers get it wrong

Plessey and GEC had a joint company in France called GPT. When this is pronounced in French, it comes out as Jay-Pay-Tay, which sounds like *J'ai pété*, meaning 'I have farted'.

KFC's 'finger-lickin' good' slogan was translated into Chinese as 'Eat your fingers off'.

Electrolux was obliged to abandon its slogan 'Nothing sucks like Electrolux'.

The lager Coors had the slogan 'Turn it loose' which, when translated into Spanish, became 'Suffer from diarrhoea'.

Pepsi-Cola had the slogan 'Come alive with the Pepsi generation' which, when translated into Chinese, became 'Pepsi brings your ancestors back from the grave'.

A Nike TV commercial for hiking shoes was shot in Kenya using Samburu tribesmen, one of whom was caught mouthing – in native Maa – 'I don't want these. Give me big shoes.'

The name Coca-Cola was, at first, Ke-kou-ke-la in Chinese until the company discovered that the phrase means 'Bite the wax tadpole' or 'Female horse stuffed with wax', depending on the dialect.

When Braniff boasted about its seats in Spanish, what should have read 'Fly in leather' became 'Fly naked'.

The German hardware store chain Götzen opened a mall in Turkey but had to change the name as *göt* means 'bum' in Turkish.

The Italian mineral water Traficante means 'drug dealer' in Spanish.

Ford had a problem in Latin American countries with their Fiera, which means 'ugly old woman' there.

Nissan launched the Moco before discovering that *moco* is the Spanish for 'mucus'.

Samarin, a Swedish remedy for upset stomachs, ran an ad that was a series of three pictures. The first was of a man looking sick, the second was of him drinking a glass of Samarin and the third was of him smiling. The company ran the ad in Arabic newspapers – where people read from right to left.

Bacardi brought out a fruit drink which they named Pavian, but, alas, *Pavian* means 'baboon' in German.

When Gerber first started selling baby food in Africa, they used their standard packaging with the cute baby on the label. They were obliged to change it when they discovered that, in Africa, the standard practice is to put pictures of the contents on foods.

Jolly Green Giant translated into Arabic means 'Intimidating Green Ogre'.

The Rolls-Royce Silver Mist range had to be renamed for the German market because *Mist* means 'dung' in German.

Genuine products

Sor Bits (Danish mints), **Krapp** (Scandinavian toilet paper), **Nora Knackers** (Norwegian biscuits), **Moron** (Italian wine), **Mukki** (Italian yoghurt), **Plopp** (Swedish toffee bar), **Bum** (Turkish biscuits), **Zit** (Greek fizzy drink), **Bimbo Bread** (Spain, South America), **Craps Chocolate** (France).

Famous men with photographic memories

Gérard Depardieu
Bill Clinton
Bill Gates
Wolfgang Amadeus Mozart

Friday the 13th

The fear of the number 13 – or 'triskaidekaphobia', as it's technically known – goes back a long way. According to Scandinavian mythology, there was a banquet in Valhalla into which Loki (the God of Strife) intruded – thereby making 13 guests – where Balder (the God of Light) was murdered. In Christian countries, this superstition was confirmed by the Last Supper.

Meanwhile, Friday is considered unlucky because it was the day of the Crucifixion and because Adam and Eve ate the forbidden fruit

on a Friday and also died on a Friday. **Some Buddhists and Brahmins (high caste Hindus) also consider Friday to be unlucky.**

Composer Arnold Schoenberg suffered from triskaidekaphobia. He died 13 minutes before midnight on Friday the 13th.

Sir Winston Churchill, the former British Prime Minister, never travelled on a Friday the 13th unless it was absolutely essential.

Graham Chapman, the late member of the Monty Python team, actually liked Friday the 13ths. Indeed, he arranged to be buried on the 13th hour of Friday, 13th October 1989.

Months that begin on a Sunday will always have a Friday the 13th.

In 2008 there is only one Friday the 13th: in June. In 2009 there are three: in February, March, November.

People who were born on a Friday the 13th include Darius Vassell, Steve Buscemi, Sara Cox, Zoë Wanamaker, Craig Bellamy, Samantha Morton and Mary-Kate & Ashley Olsen.

Words

SOS doesn't stand for 'Save Our Ship' or 'Save Our Souls' – it was chosen in 1908 at a international conference on Morse Code because the letters S and O were easy to remember. S is dot dot dot, O is dash dash dash.

The word **CORDUROY** comes from the French *cord du roi* or 'cloth of the king'.

AFGH**ANIST**AN, **KIR**GHI**STAN** and TUV**ALU** are the only countries with three consecutive letters in their names.

RESIGN has two opposing meanings depending on its pronunciation ('to quit' and 'to sign again').

In Chinese, the words 'crisis' and 'opportunity' are the same.

UNDERGROUND and **UNDERFUND** are the only two words in the English language that begin and end with the letters 'und'.

The tennis player, **GORAN IVANISEVIC**, has the longest name of a celebrity that alternates consonants and vowels.

UNITED ARAB EMIRATES is the longest name of a country that alternates vowels and consonants.

The word **THEREIN** contains 13 words spelled with consecutive letters: the, he, her, er, here, I, there, ere, rein, re, in, therein, and herein.

UNPROSPEROUSNESS is the longest word in which no letter occurs only once.

In French, **OISEAU** (bird) is the shortest word containing all five vowels.

ULTRAREVOLUTIONARIES has each vowel exactly twice.

FACETIOUS and **ABSTEMIOUS** contain the five vowels in alphabetical order.

SUBCONTINENTAL, **UNCOMPLIMENTARY** and **DUOLITERAL** contain the five vowels in reverse alphabetical order.

PLIERS is a noun with no singular form. Other such words are: **ALMS**, **CATTLE**, **EAVES**, **TROUSERS**

and **SCISSORS** (though you can say 'a pair of trousers' and 'a pair of scissors').

ACCEDED, **BAGGAGE**, **CABBAGE**, **DEFACED**, **EFFACED** and **FEEDBAG** are seven-letter words that can be played on a musical instrument.

The word **DUDE** was coined by Oscar Wilde and his friends. It is a combination of the words 'duds' and 'attitude'.

'Hijinks' is the only word in common usage with three dotted letters in a row.

EARTHLING is first found in print in 1593. Other surprisingly old words are **SPACESHIP** (1894), **ACID RAIN** (1858), **ANTACID** (1753), **HAIRDRESSER** (1771), **MOLE** (in connection with espionage, 1622, by Sir Francis Bacon), **FUNK** (a strong smell, 1623; a state of panic, 1743), **MILKY WAY** (c. 1384, but earlier in Latin) and **MS** (used instead of Miss or Mrs, 1949).

A word we have borrowed from German – **WELTSCHMERZ**, meaning 'world weariness' – has six consonants in a row.

Octopuses*

Octopus and squid can change their skin colour. Normally brown, their skin becomes green or blue when they are under threat or trying to attract a mate.

Despite its great strength, the octopus tires easily. The oxygen-carrying component of its blood, haemocyanin, is copper-based and is less efficient than the iron-based haemoglobin of humans. A struggling octopus quickly suffers oxygen deprivation.

To us, one giant octopus looks the same as another. This might explain why divers claim to have seen the same octopus occupy a den for 10 or more years even though the creature seldom lives longer than four years.

The pupil of an octopus's eye is rectangular.

The Pacific giant octopus, the largest octopus in the world, lives for only two years, during which time it grows from the size of pea to a creature

* Or octopi, or octopodi . . .

weighing 70 kilos and measuring 9 or 10 metres across.

Because it has no backbone, a 35-kilo octopus can squeeze through a hole the size of a large coin.

Unlike humans, the octopus doesn't have a blind spot.

An octopus has three hearts.

Beds and sleep

A bed is the third most popular luxury chosen by castaways on the radio programme *Desert Island Discs* (a piano is first and 'writing materials' are second).

The expression 'to get out of bed on the wrong side' comes from the 19th-century superstition that there was a 'right' side (the right) for getting out of bed and a 'wrong' side (the left) – based, of course, on the traditional fear of anything 'left' ('sinister' being the Latin word for left).

King Louis XI of France started the practice of French kings receiving their courtiers and ministers from their bed by introducing *lit de justice* (bed of justice), a ceremonial appearance before his parliament of the king lying in bed, with his princes on stools, and with great officials standing and lesser ones kneeling.

Thomas Hobbes, the philosopher, and the writers Edith Wharton, F. Scott Fitzgerald and Marcel Proust all worked in their beds.

When John Denver lost his temper with his then wife, Annie (made famous in 'Annie's Song'), he sawed their bed in half.

More than 600,000 Americans each year are injured on beds and chairs.

The shortest recorded time taken by one person to make a bed is 28.2 seconds by Wendy Wall of Sydney, Australia, in 1978; the record time for two people to make a bed is 14 seconds by Sister Sharon Stringer and Nurse Michelle Benkel at London's Royal Masonic Hospital at the launch of the 1994 edition of *The Guinness Book of Records*.

The United States has many sleepy towns: Sleepy Eye (Minnesota), Sleepy Creek (Oregon), Sleeping Beauty Peak (Arizona), Sleepers Bend (California).

According to the philosopher Friedrich Nietzsche: 'Sleeping is no mean art. For its sake one must stay awake all day.'

American comedian Max Kauffmann reckoned that 'the amount of sleep required by the average person is about five minutes more'.

Celebrities who are also qualified pilots

John Travolta

Angelina Jolie

Sir Alan Sugar

Nicholas Lyndhurst

Prince Charles

Tom Cruise

John Grisham

Harrison Ford

Martin Shaw

Gene Hackman

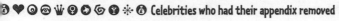

Celebrities who had their appendix removed

Kate Beckinsale

Jonny Wilkinson

Lindsay Lohan

Mel Gibson

Sir Steven Redgrave

Patsy Palmer

Sue Barker

Minnie Driver

Prince Charles

Lost in translation

According to a poll of 1,000 translators, the most untranslatable word in the world is ILUNGA, from the Bantu language of Tshiluba; it means a person ready to forgive an abuse the first time, tolerate it the second time, but neither the third time. The runners-up were:

SHLIMAZL   Yiddish for a chronically unlucky person.

RADIOUKACZ Polish for a person who worked as a telegrapher for the resistance movements on the Soviet side of the Iron Curtain.

NAA   A Japanese word used only in Kansai area of Japan for emphasis or to agree with someone.

ALTAHMAM   Arabic for a kind of deep sadness.

GEZELLIG Dutch for an atmosphere or feeling that is cosy.

SAUDADE Portuguese for a certain type of longing.

SELATHIRUPAVAR Tamil for a certain type of truancy.

POCHEMUCHKA Russian for a particular kind of person who asks a lot of questions.

KLLOSHAR Albanian for something like 'loser'.

Celebrities who have run marathons (all in London except where stated)

Gordon Ramsay

Jasper Carrott

Charlie Dimmock

Patrick Kielty

Steve Cram

Steve Rider

Jonny Lee Miller

Alastair Campbell

Lucy Benjamin

Nell McAndrew

Sir Ranulph Fiennes

Richard Herring

Kate Garraway

Lorraine Kelly

Sean 'P Diddy' Combs (NY)

Katie Holmes (NY)

Will Ferrell (Boston)

Oprah Winfrey (Marine Corps)

Birds

Male cockatoos have black irises and invisible pupils; the females have paler irises with visible pupils.

The ostrich yolk is the largest single cell in the world.

Some birds have eyes that weigh more than their brains.

Wandering albatrosses devote a full year to raising their young.

An owl can see a mouse 50 metres away in light no brighter than a candle-flame.

The heaviest flighted birds in the world are the great bustard at 18 kilos, the trumpeter swan at 16.5 kilos, the mute swan at 16 kilos, the albatross and the whooper swan at 15.5 kilos.

Penguins have an organ above their eyes that converts seawater into fresh water.

Wild turkeys are fast on the ground, running at speeds of up to 30 mph (50 kph).

The male wren builds several nests as part of his courtship ritual. Once the nests are completed, his potential bride looks them all over, then selects one in which to lay her eggs.

Migrating geese fly in a V-formation to conserve energy. The wings churn the air and create a current. In the flying wedge, each bird is in position to get lift from the current created by the bird ahead. It is easier going for all, except the leader. During a migration, geese take turns in the lead position.

The weaverbird, found in Africa and India, builds elaborate nests. The female weaverbird will refuse to mate with a male if his nest is not good enough. If she rejects the nest, he must take it apart and rebuild it.

Grebes can plunge 30 metres down into the water and can stay under for as long as three minutes. There, they snare fish, which they swallow alive, head first.

Bald eagles can swim. They use an overarm movement of their wings that is like the butterfly stroke. They also build the biggest nests. One found was 3 metres wide and 6 metres deep.

A flock of starlings flies in loose formation – until a falcon appears. Then the flock tightens up so the falcon doesn't have a single bird to strike at.

The duck-billed platypus of Australia can store up to 600 worms in its cheek pouches.

The female condor lays one egg every two years.

The hummingbird, the kingfisher and the grebe are all birds that cannot walk.

Reptiles

In Africa more people are killed by crocodiles than by lions.

From crocodile farms, Australia exports about 5,000 crocodile skins a year. Most go to Paris, where a crocodile handbag can sell for more than £5,000.

The Nile crocodile lives for about 45 years in the wild, and up to 80 years in captivity.

A baby crocodile is three times as long as the egg it has hatched from.

Alligators cannot move backwards.

Turtles can live for more than 100 years; some have been known to live to 150. They never die of old age – once their bodies reach maturity, they stop changing.

Whether a sea turtle is male or female depends on the temperature of the sand in which it incubated as an egg. Warm temperatures (greater than 29°C) produce more females; cooler temperatures (less than 29°C) produce more males.

An alligator can go through 2,000 to 3,000 teeth in a lifetime.

Celebrities

Sheryl Crow's front two teeth are fake – her own were knocked out when she tripped on stage.

Jordan is keen on sewing.

Daniel Craig's middle name is Wroughton.

The artist Vincent van Gogh cut off his left ear. His _Self-portrait with Bandaged Ear_ shows the right one bandaged because he painted the mirror image.

David Beckham and George Clooney are both keen cartoonists.

James Woods, Dick Van Dyke and Maria Sharapova are all ambidextrous – that's to say, they can do things equally well with either hand.

Olivia Newton-John is president of the Isle of Man Basking Sharks Society.

Nick Nolte ate real dog food in the film _Down and Out in Beverly Hills_ (when he was showing

the dog how to eat from a dog bowl).

Sir Winston Churchill smoked an estimated 300,000 cigars in his lifetime.

Pierce Brosnan bought the typewriter of James Bond creator Ian Fleming for £52,800.

Tommy Lee has a Starbucks in his house.

Kim Basinger puts sour cream and lemon juice in her bath water.

Marlon Brando's occupation on his passport was 'Shepherd'.

Julio Iglesias once had five gallons of water flown from Miami to LA so he could wash his hair.

Michael Jackson owns the rights to the South Carolina state anthem.

Simon Le Bon has kept bees.

Debra Winger was the voice of ET.

Dusty Springfield once successfully sued Bobby Davro for an imitation he did of her.

Woody Allen won't take a shower if the drain is in the middle.

Alan Davies bought the original Big Brother diary room chair for £30,000.

Queen Latifah wears the key for the motorcycle on which her brother suffered a fatal crash on a chain round her neck.

Mel C, David Beckham, Amanda Holden and Boris Johnson all salute magpies (as a superstition).

Robert Downey Jr once spent a night in jail with Tommy Lee.

Cate Blanchett gave her husband plaster casts of her ears as a present.

Arm-wrestling is one of Helena Bonham Carter's favourite pastimes.

Renée Zellweger keeps a 'grateful journal' – a collection of her favourite things – on her bedside table.

Sean 'P. Diddy' Combs wears a diamond-encrusted watch to protect against pollution from his mobile phone.

Nicolas Cage was 28 before he first went abroad (to a screening in Cannes). He employs his own pizza chef and has a special pizza oven in his house.

During their marriage, Angelina Jolie and Billy Bob Thornton bought an electric chair for their dining room.

Gisele Bundchen owns over 200 belts.

Missy Elliott spends four hours a day on her hair.

Diane Keaton's old college named a street after her in 2000.

Harrison Ford has a species of spider named after him.

Chips

In Britain the first mention of chips is to be found in an 1854 recipe book, *Shilling Cookery*, in which chef Alexis Soyer referred to a recipe with 'thin cut potatoes cooked in oil'.

In 1857 author Charles Dickens referred to plates of 'potato sticks cooked in oil'.

Gram for gram, chips contain a quarter of the fat of doughnuts.

The British eat over 2 million tonnes of chips every year – that's 37 kilos for each person every year.

Chips are the biggest-selling frozen vegetable in the world.

There are 8,500 fish and chip shops the UK. In the 1950s there were more than 30,000. Nevertheless, chippies are still the most popular take-away restaurants in the UK.

In Britain 57 per cent of people put vinegar on our chips; 24 per cent tomato ketchup; 8 per cent brown sauce; 5 per cent mayonnaise and 2 per cent gravy.

Only the British sprinkle their chips with vinegar. The French usually have a pinch of salt, the Belgians use mayonnaise, while the Americans use tomato ketchup.

At the largest frozen chip factory in Britain, 3.5 tonnes of potatoes are processed every hour.

In 1996 the Irish introduced edible bags for chips to cut down on litter. According to someone who ate one, the bags 'taste a bit like mashed potato'.

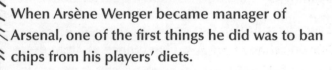

When Arsène Wenger became manager of Arsenal, one of the first things he did was to ban chips from his players' diets.

American *Vogue* ran into trouble when it published a recipe that recommended using horse lard to cook tastier French fries.

80 per cent of the British population visit fish and chip shops at least once a year. 22 per cent go at least once a week.

In the 19th century fish and chip fryers were social outcasts because of the strong odour of frying that stuck to their clothes.

Chippies officially remained an offensive trade until 1940. If the fat was not changed every day, the shops smelled awful and were usually confined to the poorer districts of town. As their popularity grew, however, the equipment and premises became more sophisticated.

Chips are a good source of vitamin C and complex carbohydrates in the form of starch. They also provide protein, fibre, iron and other vitamins.

Every year British fish and chip shops chop up 500,000 tons of potatoes for chips – that's one twelfth of all the potatoes eaten in Britain.

The Germans have invented a revolutionary oven that produces a greaseless chip.

According to her mother, Carol Vorderman and her siblings were fed chips every day.

The actress Cameron Diaz says she has a 'love affair with French fries', which plays havoc with her skin. 'I've always been a salty, greasy kind of girl,' she declares.

Nick Faldo shocked the American golfing establishment when he ordered chips for the 1997 Masters dinner. As defending champion, it was up to him to choose the menu for the Past Champions dinner in the Augusta National clubhouse. After his two previous victories, he had chosen steak and kidney pie and shepherd's pie, but in 1997 he selected British fish, chips and, of course, mushy peas.

If...

If **Holly Hunter** married **George W. Bush**, she'd be Holly Bush.

If **Cat Deeley** married **Jamie Foxx**, she'd be Cat Foxx.

If **Iman** married **Gary Oldman**, she'd be Iman Oldman.

If **Cherie Blair** married **Oliver Stone**, she'd be Cherie Stone.

If **Lindsay Lohan** married **Robert Lindsay**, she'd be Lindsay Lindsay.

If **Minnie Driver** married **Alice Cooper**, she'd be Minnie Cooper.

If **Sandi Toksvig** married **Pauly Shore**, she'd be Sandi Shore.

If **Olivia Newton-John** married **Wayne Newton**, then divorced him to marry **Elton John**, she'd be Olivia Newton-John Newton John.

Three wise monkeys

Mizaru (see no evil)

Mikazaru (hear no evil)

Mazaru (say no evil)

The most beautiful words in the English language

In 2004, to mark its 70th anniversary, the British Council asked 7,000 people in 46 countries what they considered to be the most beautiful words in the English language. There was also an online poll that attracted over 35,000 votes. Here are the top 20:

1. Mother
2. Passion
3. Smile
4. Love
5. Eternity
6. Fantastic
7. Destiny
8. Freedom
9. Liberty
10. Tranquillity
11. Peace
12. Blossom

13. Sunshine
14. Sweetheart
15. Gorgeous
16. Cherish
17. Enthusiasm
18. Hope
19. Grace
20. Rainbow

Famous people and what they're allergic to

Brad Pitt – dogs
Lindsay Lohan – blueberries
Lenny Henry – chicken
Richard E. Grant – alcohol
Clint Eastwood – horses

Drew Barrymore – garlic, bee stings, perfume and coffee

Naomi Campbell – tuna

Trisha Goddard – lactose: chocolate, milk or dairy products

Tom Cruise – cats

Ulrika Jonsson – pine trees

Dannii Minogue – wheat, dairy products and yeast

Sandra Bullock – horses

Tony Robinson – red wine, cats and feathers

Ross Kemp – wasps

Lleyton Hewitt – grass, horses and cats

Gail Porter – oil

Ioan Gruffudd – cats

Gareth Gates – oranges, coffee and cheese

Gillian Anderson – cat hair

Alistair McGowan – wig glue

Oxymorons?

Army intelligence, **civil servant**, easy payments, **working lunch**, corporate hospitality, **friendly fire**, executive decision, **operator service**, guest host, **business ethics**, virtual reality, **jumbo shrimp**, committee decision, **same difference**, free trade, **student teacher**, airline food, **floppy disk**, civil disobedience, **working holiday**, crash landing, **educated guess**, martial law, **paid volunteer**

History

Alfred Nobel invented dynamite; his father, Emmanuel, invented plywood.

In Sweden in the Middle Ages, a mayor was once elected by a louse. The candidates rested their beards on a table and the louse was placed in the middle. The louse's chosen host became mayor.

Legend has it that after he was beheaded, St Denis, the patron saint of Paris, carried his head around and walked for some distance.

During the Second World War, the American automobile industry produced just 139 cars.

During the Crusades, the difficulty of transporting bodies off the battlefield for burial was resolved by taking out a huge cauldron, boiling down the bodies and removing the bones.

Spanish doubloons (coins) were legal tender in the US until 1857.

For 3,000 years, until 1883, hemp was the world's largest agricultural crop, from which the majority of fabric was produced.

Queen Anne died in 1714. All 18 of her children (including 13 miscarriages) had died before her.

Lady Macbeth had a son called Lulach the Fatuous.

Sultan Murad IV inherited 240 wives when he assumed the throne of Turkey in 1744. He put each wife into a sack and tossed them one by one into the Bosphorus.

During the Second World War it was against the law in Germany to name a horse Adolf.

Napoleon constructed his battle plans in a sandbox.

The author Mark Twain was born on a day in 1835 when Haley's Comet came into view. When he died in 1910, Haley's Comet came into view again.

The dog and the turkey were the only two domesticated animals in ancient Mexico.

The Pentagon has twice as many toilets as necessary because in the 1940s, when it was built, Virginia still had segregation laws requiring separate facilities for blacks and whites.

The Puritans took three times as much beer as water with them on their journey to the New World.

In ancient Japan a man could divorce his wife if he discovered that she was left-handed.

In 14th-century France a pig was executed by public hanging for the murder of a child.

Abraham Lincoln held an alcohol licence and ran several taverns.

In the 1600s thermometers were filled with brandy instead of mercury.

A quarter of the horses in the US died in a virus epidemic in 1872.

An earthquake on 16 December 1811 caused parts of the Mississippi river to flow backwards.

Lipsticks changed from potted paints to bullet-shaped tubes during the First World War.

The skin of sharks was once sold and used as sandpaper.

Napoleon Bonaparte is the historical figure most often portrayed in movies.

The ancient Ottoman Empire once had seven emperors in seven months. They died of (in order): burning, choking, drowning, stabbing, heart failure, poisoning and being thrown from a horse.

The turkey was once a sacred bird. Aztec emperor Montezuma used to receive 1,000 turkeys a day from his subjects as tributes.

During the 1800s swan skins were used to make European ladies' powder puffs and swan feathers were used to adorn fashionable hats.

The electric razor was invented by Jacob Schick. During the First World War he was in the US army, serving in Alaska. Tired of breaking the layer of ice that formed in the washbasin so that he could shave, he developed the first hand-held motor, which he patented in 1923. In 1931 he finished his razor and it was on the market for $25. By 1937 he'd sold nearly 2 million.

How to write

Steer well clear of clichés; give them a wide berth.

Do not be redundant; do not use more words to express an idea or concept than you really need to use.

All verbs has to agree with subjects.

Always avoid annoying alliteration.

Be specific, more or less.

Parenthetical remarks (however pertinent) are (almost certainly) superfluous.

Complete sentences only, please.

The passive voice is to be avoided.

Foreign words and phrases are de trop.

Delete commas, that are, not necessary.

One should never generalize.

Avoid ampersands & abbreviations, etc.

Analogies in writing are like pyjamas on a cat.

Never use a big word where a diminutive expression would suffice.

Eliminate quotations. As Ralph Waldo Emerson said, 'I hate quotations.'

A mixed metaphor, even one that flies like a bird, should be given its marching orders.

Who needs rhetorical questions?

Exaggeration is a million times worse than understatement.

Proofread carefully to see if you any words out.

Mnemonics and aides-memoire

The plants in order of distance from the Sun: Mercury, Venus, Earth, Mars, Jupiter, Saturn, Uranus, Neptune, Pluto – **My Very Easy Method: Just Set Up Nine Planets**.

The order of colours in the rainbow: Red, Orange, Yellow, Green, Blue, Indigo, Violet – **Richard Of York Gave Battle In Vain**.

The order of sharps in music: FCGDAEB – **Father Charles Goes Down And Ends Battle**.

The order of notes to which guitar strings should be tuned: EBGDAE – **Easter Bunnies Get Drunk At Easter**.

The order of notes represented by the lines

on the treble clef stave: EGBDF – **Every Good Boy Deserves Favour**.

The four oceans: Indian, Arctic, Atlantic, Pacific – **I Am A Person**.

The Great Lakes: Huron, Ontario, Michigan, Erie, Superior – **HOMES**. For the Great Lakes in order of size: Superior, Huron, Michigan, Erie, Ontario – **Sam's Horse Must Eat Oats**.

Famous nailbiters

Gordon Brown
Orlando Bloom
Dustin Hoffman
Liza Minnelli
Steven Spielberg
Cate Blanchett
Britney Spears (after
hypnosis failed,
she painted her
nails with a red-hot
pepper polish that
burned her tongue)
Mel B (toenails)
Will Young
Elijah Wood
Emilia Fox
Melanie Sykes
Jamie Theakston
Louis Theroux

Written by drivers on insurance forms

'I didn't think the speed limit applied after midnight.'

'I consider that neither car was to blame, but if either one was to blame, it would be the other one.'

'I knocked over a man. He admitted it was his fault as he had been run over before.'

'Coming home I drove into the wrong house and collided with a tree I don't have.'

'The other car collided with mine without giving warning of its intentions.'

'In my attempt to kill a fly, I drove into a telephone pole.'

'I had been driving for 40 years when I fell asleep at the wheel and had an accident.'

'I was thrown from my car as it left the road, and was later found in a ditch by some stray cows.'

'The guy was all over the road. I had to swerve a number of times before I hit him.'

'An invisible car came out of nowhere, struck my car and vanished.'

'The accident happened because I had one eye on the lorry in front, one eye on the pedestrian and the other on the car behind.'

The claimant had collided with a cow. Question: 'What warning was given by you?' Answer: 'Horn.' Question: 'What warning was given by the other party?' Answer: 'Moo.'

'The car in front hit the pedestrian but he got up so I hit him again.'

'The pedestrian ran for the pavement, but I got him.'

'If the other driver had stopped a few yards behind himself the accident would not have happened.'

'A lamp-post bumped the car, damaging it in two places.'

'I left my car unattended for a minute and, whether by accident or design, it ran away.'

Science and nature

A combustion engine wastes 75 per cent of the chemical energy contained in petrol.

The liquid inside young coconuts can be used as a substitute for blood plasma.

The Siberian larch accounts for more than 20 per cent of the world's trees.

There is cyanide in apple pips.

If you put a raisin in a glass of champagne, it will keep floating to the top and sinking to the bottom.

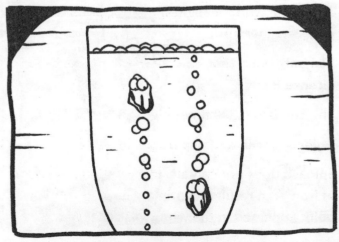

Cranberries are one of just three major fruits native to North America. Blueberries and Concord grapes are the other two.

The average iceberg weighs 20 million tons.

The Chinese were using aluminium as early as AD300. Western civilization didn't rediscover it until 1827.

The angle between the branches and the trunk of a tree is constant from one member to another of the same species of tree.

It takes 4,000 crocuses to produce 25 grams of saffron.

The metal with the highest melting point is tungsten, at 3,410°C.

The only thing that can destroy a diamond is intense heat.

The Sun is 300,300 times bigger than the Earth.

Onions, garlic and asparagus are lilies.

Spinach does not contain an exceptional amount of iron. As a result of a printing error, the decimal point appeared in the wrong place. However, spinach does contain useful amounts of iron and is very good for you.

There is no such thing as a banana tree. Bananas grow on plants.

Bone china is so called because powdered animal bone is mixed with the clay to give the finished china translucency and whiteness.

The estimated temperature at the centre of the Earth is around 4,100°C.

30,000 monkeys were used in the massive three-year effort to classify the various types of polio.

There are 20,000 living organisms in a glass of water.

The average hailstorm lasts about 15 minutes.

A comet's tail always points away from the Sun.

Gemstones contain several elements – except the diamond, which is all carbon.

Misquotations

'Alas, poor Yorick, I knew him well.'

'Alas poor Yorick! I knew him, Horatio.'
(Hamlet in *Hamlet* by William Shakespeare)

'A little knowledge is a dangerous thing.'

'A little learning is a dangerous thing.'
(Alexander Pope)

'Money is the root of all evil.'

'For the love of money is the root of all evil.'
(The Bible – Timothy 6:10)

'Elementary, my dear Watson.'

'Elementary.'
(Sherlock Holmes to Dr Watson
in Sir Arthur Conan Doyle's stories)

'Hubble bubble, toil and trouble.'

'Double double, toil and trouble.'
(The witches in *Macbeth* by William Shakespeare)

'To gild the lily.'

'To gild refined gold, to paint the lily.'
(The Earl of Salisbury in *King John* by William
Shakespeare)

'Me Tarzan, you Jane.'

Tarzan and Jane pointed at themselves and each
said their own name in *Tarzan the Ape Man*.

'When in Rome do as the Romans do.'

'If you are at Rome, live after the Roman fashion;
if you are elsewhere, live as they do there.'
(St Ambrose)

Animals

Sea otters inhabit water but never get wet skin because they have two coats of fur.

There is a strong bond between mother and child among orangutans. An orangutan infant will cling to its mother until it is almost two years old.

The average koala sleeps 22 hours a day.

A baby caribou is so swift it can outrun its mother when it is only three days old.

Giraffes are the only animals born with horns. Both males and females are born with bony knobs on the forehead.

The definition of a 'mammal' is that the female animal feeds her young on milk she has produced.

A horse eats about seven times its own weight each year.

The male moose sheds its antlers every winter and grows a new set the following year.

Until they were imported into the country, Australia had no members of the cat family, no hoofed animals and no apes or monkeys.

Skunks protect themselves by giving out a pungent and foul smell. They have other means of protection too. They can withstand five times the snake venom that would kill a rabbit.

Wild cats hold their tail horizontally, or tucked between their legs, when walking.

Not all male lions have manes. Some have no more than a slight ruff around their cheeks.

A giraffe can kill a lion with just one kick.

The biggest members of the cat family are Siberian and Bengal tigers.

A full-grown kangaroo can be taller than a man.

Among Asian elephants, only the males have tusks. Both sexes of African elephants have tusks.

Elephants use leafy branches and plant stalks as fly swatters.

The elephant's closest relative is the hyrax, which is found in the Middle East and Africa. The tiny creature is about 30 cm long. Like its gigantic cousin, the hyrax has hoofed toes and a two-chambered stomach for digesting a vegetable diet.

An adult cheetah's tail can be 80 cm long.

A male kangaroo is called a boomer. A female kangaroo is called a flyer.

An elephant produces about 20 kilos of dung a day.

Famous people who lived in their cars

Jim Carrey (at one point his family lived out of their car/trailer)

Roger Daltrey (used to live in a van)

Brad Pitt

Chris Tarrant

Lenny Kravitz (a Ford Pinto)

Hilary Swank (with her mother when she was a kid)

Bob Hoskins (in a jeep after an expensive divorce)

The human condition

Your foot is the same length as the distance between your wrist and your elbow.

The chemicals in a human body are estimated to have a combined worth of 6.25 euros.

Humans are the only animals that cry.

It takes just one minute for blood to travel through the whole human body.

The first of the five senses to go with age is smell.

You can't kill yourself by holding your breath.

Right-handed people live, on average, nine years longer than left-handed people do.

Humans are the only primates that don't have pigment in the palms of their hands.

If you farted continuously for six years and nine months, enough wind would be produced to equal the energy of an atomic bomb.

Banging your head against a wall uses 150 calories an hour.

We get goose pimples where our ancestors used to have hair.

The average person has 100,000 hairs on his or her head – but redheads have fewer and blondes have more.

A baby cries without tears until it's three months old.

The hardest substance in your body is the enamel in your teeth.

Taste is 75 per cent smell.

BOOOOM!

There are four basic tastes: sweet, salty, sour and bitter.

The colour blue can have a calming effect.

Red blood cells, created in the bone marrow, go round the body 250,000 times before returning to the bone marrow to be destroyed.

Within a tiny droplet of blood, there are some 5 million red blood cells.

Hair is easier to cut after being soaked in warm water.

An olfactory receptor cell is something that helps us to smell smells. The average human has 40 million of these cells. The average rabbit has 100 million. The average dog has 1 billion.

A guide to 'strine' (Australian slang)

Bonza or **beaut** = wonderful, great

Tucker = food

Wowser = killjoy, spoilsport

Cobber = mate

Chook = chicken (as eaten on a 'barbie')

Crook = unwell (as in 'strewth, I'm crook')

Dead as a dead dingo = in a parlous condition

Dunny = toilet

Fair dinkum = the real thing (sometimes uttered in spite of oneself, as in, 'Fair dinkum, that bloke can bat')

Fair go = good chance (as in 'Shane's got a fair go of taking a wicket against these poms)

Godzone – God's own country (i.e. Australia)

Hit your kick = open your wallet (as in 'come on, blue, hit your kick and pay for those tinnies')

Hooly dooly = I say! (as in 'Hooly dooly, have you seen the state of that dunny?')

Ripper = super

A sausage short of a barbie = not in possession of all (his) faculties

Spit the dummy (to) = lose one's cool (as in 'I think he's spitting the dummy')

Unusual deaths

Chrysippus (philosopher): In 207BC, he is believed to have died of laughter after watching his drunken donkey try to eat figs.

Attila the Hun (warrior): In 453 he bled to death from a nosebleed on his wedding night.

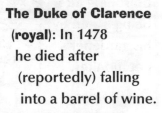

The Duke of Clarence (royal): In 1478 he died after (reportedly) falling into a barrel of wine.

Sir Francis Bacon (philosopher and statesman): In 1626 he died from pneumonia caught when experimenting with freezing a chicken by stuffing it with snow.

William Huskisson (politician): In 1830 he became the first person to be killed by a train. The accident happened when he was attending

the opening of the Liverpool–Manchester Railway. As he stepped onto the track to meet the Duke of Wellington, Stephenson's *Rocket* hit him.

Allan Pinkerton (detective): In 1884 he died of gangrene as a result of biting his tongue after stumbling on the pavement.

King Alexander I of Greece: In 1920 he died from blood poisoning after being bitten by his gardener's pet monkey.

Frank Hayes (jockey): In 1923 he died from a heart attack during a race. His horse went on to finish first – making him the only dead jockey to win a race.

Isadora Duncan (dancer): In 1927 she was strangled when her scarf was caught in the spokes of a car's wheel.

Jerome Napoleon Bonaparte (the last member of the famous Bonaparte family): In 1945 he died of the injuries he sustained after tripping over his dog's lead.

Alex Mitchell (bricklayer): In 1975 he died laughing at a sketch on the TV show *The Goodies*.

Tennessee Williams (playwright): In 1983 he choked to death on a nose-spray bottle cap that dropped into his mouth while he was using the spray.

Garry Hoy (lawyer): In 1993 he died after throwing himself through the glass wall on the 24th floor of the Toronto-Dominion Centre in order to prove the glass was 'unbreakable'. It wasn't.

Appeared in pop videos

Elijah Wood – 'Ridiculous Thought' by
The Cranberries

Matt Lucas – 'Country House' by Blur

Johnny Depp – 'Into the
Wide Great Open'
by Tom Petty

Benicio Del Toro
– *'La Isla Bonita'* by
Madonna

Jamie Bell – 'Wake Me
Up When September Ends'
by Green Day

Sir Ian McKellen – 'Heart'
by the Pet Shop Boys

Phill Jupitus
– 'Happy Hour' by
The Housemartins

Naomi Campbell
– 'I'll Tumble for Ya'
by Culture Club

Michelle Pfeiffer – 'Gangsta's Paradise' by Coolio

Angelina Jolie – 'Rock & Roll Dreams Come Through' by Meat Loaf

Tamzin Outhwaite – 'Even Better Than the Real Thing' by U2

Claudia Schiffer – 'Uptown Girl' by Westlife

George Clooney – 'She's Just Killin' Me' by ZZ Top

Daryl Hannah – 'Feel' by Robbie Williams (she thought she was going to be working with *Robin* Williams)

Kirsten Dunst – 'I Knew I Loved You' by Savage Garden

Carmen Electra – 'We Are All Made of Stars' by Moby

Denise Van Outen – 'Proper Crimbo' by Avid Merrion

Jennifer Lopez – 'That's the Way Love Goes' by Janet Jackson

Wesley Snipes – 'Bad' by Michael Jackson

Eggs

The tradition of decorating eggs at Easter
started thousands of years ago to celebrate the
return of spring after a hard winter.
Eggs symbolize new life.

**Eggs in Britain are mostly eaten
boiled. Second most popular is
scrambled, and third is fried.**

You can tell an egg is fresh
if it sinks to the bottom of a
pan of water. Eggs take in air
as they age, so an old egg floats
more easily.

**Crushed eggshells sprinkled round
lettuce plants should help to stop
insects nibbling the leaves.**

Hens lay, in peak production,
one egg a day.

**In parts of France brides
break an egg for luck before
they enter their new home.**

In a court of law in Basle, Switzerland, in 1471, a cockerel was found guilty of laying an egg 'in defiance of natural law'. The bird was burned at the stake as a 'devil in disguise'.

Paul Newman's character in *Cool Hand Luke* eats 50 hard-boiled eggs.

The USA

Cats are the most popular pets in America. Altogether there are 66 million pet cats, 58 million pet dogs and 14 million pet parakeets in the United States. There are also between 5,000 and 7,000 pet tigers.

About 18 per cent of American pet owners share their beds with their pets.

99 per cent of the pumpkins sold in the US end up as jack-o'-lanterns.

In 1965 Congress authorized the Secret Service to protect former presidents and their spouses for their lifetime, unless they decline the protection. Recently, Congress limited the protection of former presidents and their spouses (elected after 1 January 1997) to 10 years after leaving office. President Clinton, who was elected in 1996, will be the last president to receive lifelong protection from the Secret Service.

The average American bank teller loses about $250 every year.

A typical American eats 28 pigs in a lifetime.

32 per cent of all the land in the US is owned by the government.

The motto of the American people, 'In God We Trust', was not adopted as the national slogan until 1956.

In 1935 the police in Atlantic City, New Jersey, arrested 42 men on the beach. They were cracking down on topless bathing suits worn by men.

The American authorities allow an average of 30 or more insect fragments and one or more rodent hairs per 100 grams of peanut butter.

Pepsi-Cola was created by Caleb Bradham in 1902 from a mixture of oil, spices, vanilla, sugar and an enzyme called pepsin.

The White House, in Washington, DC, was originally grey, the colour of the sandstone it was built from. After the War of 1812, during which it had been burned by Canadian troops, the outside walls were painted white to hide the smoke stains.

People who gave their names to things

Laszlo Bíró – Biro

Count Stroganoff – Beef Stroganoff

Charles Boycott – Boycott

Louis Braille – Braille

Robert Bunsen – Bunsen Burner

Rudolf Diesel – Diesel

Commodore Benedict – Eggs Benedict

George Ferris – Ferris wheel

Sir William Gage – Greengage

Jules Léotard – Leotard

Ned Ludd – Luddite

John Macadam – Macadamia nut

Samuel Maverick – Maverick

Franz Mesmer – Mesmerize

Jean Nicot – Nicotine

Anna Pavlova – Pavlova

Adolphe Sax – Saxophone

Earl Silas Tupper – Tupperware

Cats

There are over 6 million cats in the UK, where the most popular breeds are Persian long hair, Siamese and British short hair. The collective name for a group of cats is a 'clowder'.

The average lifespan of a cat is between 13 and 17 years (depending on the breed and the gender), although one cat reached the age of 34.

The largest cat litter recorded is 19 – although four were still-born.

The ragdoll is the largest breed of domesticated cat in the world.

The most popular names for British cats are
Sooty, Kitty, Tiger, Tigger, Charlie, Molly, Oscar
and Smoky.

The normal body temperature of a cat is 38.6°C.

All cats step with both left legs, then both right legs,
when they walk or run. The only other animals to do
this are the giraffe and the camel.

There isn't a single reference to a cat in the Bible.

Famous cat lovers in history include author
Raymond Chandler, Dr Samuel Johnson and Sir
Winston Churchill, the former prime minister,
who used to sleep with his cat in the bed next
to him.

The domestic cat is the only species of cat able to hold its tail vertically while walking.

Famous cat haters include composer Johannes Brahms, the Queen, French dictator Napoleon Bonaparte, James Boswell (Dr Johnson's biographer) and Batman (professionally only).

Domestic cats purr at about 26 cycles per second, the same frequency as an idling diesel engine.

The people of East Anglia used to mummify cats and place them in the walls of their homes to ward off evil spirits.

Since housecats are clean and their coats are dry and glossy, their fur easily becomes charged with electricity. Sparks can sometimes be seen if their fur is rubbed in the dark.

Cats need to consume a substance called tryptophan, which is found in milk, eggs and poultry, in order to sleep well. Without it, they can become insomniacs.

Proportional to their size, cats have the largest eyes of all mammals.

4,000 years ago in Egypt, the penalty for killing a cat was death.

During the Second World War a cat named Oscar served on the German battleship *Bismarck*. When the *Bismarck* was torpedoed, Oscar was rescued by a British sailor from HMS *Cossack*. Five months later HMS *Cossack* was sunk but Oscar was rescued by HMS *Ark Royal*. Just three weeks later a German U-boat destroyed the *Ark Royal* and Oscar was rescued again. Oscar was then left to live on land and died peacefully many years later.

Books

John Milton used 8,000 different words in *Paradise Lost*.

The first novel, *The Tale of Genji*, was written in 1007 by a Japanese noblewoman, Murasaki Shikibu.

The world's longest non-fiction work is *The Yongle Dadian*, a 10,000-volume encyclopedia produced by 5,000 scholars during the Chinese Ming Dynasty 600 years ago.

Greek philosopher Aristotle wrote Meteology in the 4th century BC: it remained the standard textbook on weather for 2,000 years.

The first illustrated book for children – *The Treasure of Siegfried* – was published in Germany in 1658.

The main library at Indiana University sinks by several centimetres a year. When it was built, no one took into account the weight of all the books it would hold.

Some famous people and their favourite children's book

Dawn French: *The Hobbit*

Tony Blair: *Kidnapped*

Sir Alex Ferguson: *Treasure Island*

Lorraine Kelly: *Just So Stories*

Eamonn Holmes: *The Lion, the Witch and the Wardrobe*

Chris Evans: *Black Beauty*

Professor Stephen Hawking: *She*

Sir David Attenborough: *The Bird of Paradise*

Steven Spielberg: *Treasure Island*

Jamie Foxx: *Green Eggs and Ham*

Courtney Cox: *The Velveteen Rabbit*

Numbers

In the US, a centillion is the number 1 followed by 300 zeros. In Britain it has 600 zeros.

There are 318,979,564,000 possible combinations of the first four moves in chess.

Any number squared is equal to one more than the numbers on either side of it multiplied together – 5 x 5 = 25 and 4 x 6 = 24; 6 x 6 = 36 and 5 x 7 = 35 etc.

Any number squared is equal to 4 (2 squared) more than the product of the numbers that lie two away from it:

> 5 squared is 25 (3 x 7 = 21)

> 8 squared is 64 (6 x 10 = 60)

Any number squared is equal to 9 (3 squared) more than the product of the numbers that lie three away from it:

> 5 squared is 25 (2 x 8 = 16)

> 8 squared is 64 (5 x 11 = 55, and so on).

There are **1,929,770,126,028,800** different colour combinations possible on a Rubik's Cube.

The smallest number with **three** letters is 1 (one)

. . . with **four** letters is 4 (four).

. . . with **five** letters is 3 (three).

. . . with **six** letters is 11 (eleven).

. . . with **seven** letters is 15 (fifteen).

. . . with **eight** letters is 13 (thirteen).

. . . with **nine** letters is 17 (seventeen).

. . . with **ten** letters is 24 (twenty-four).

Keen Scrabble players

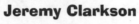

Madonna

Jennifer Aniston

Will Smith

Jo Brand

Norman Cook (Fatboy Slim)

Robbie Williams

Delia Smith

Jeremy Clarkson

Jonathan Ross

Kylie Minogue

Brad Pitt

Ant

Dec

Damon Albarn

Mel Gibson

Chris Martin

Alistair McGowan

Sean Hughes

Keen cyclists

Madonna

Jon Snow

Brad Pitt

Alexei Sayle

Jeremy Paxman

Boris Johnson

Mena Suvari

Olivia Williams

Robin Williams

Snakes

There are only three types of snake on the island of Tasmania and all are deadly poisonous.

The longest snake is the royal python, which can grow to 10.6 metres.

Most snakes breathe with only one lung. The left lung is either reduced in size or missing completely.

When they're fighting, tree snakes try to swallow each other.

Sidewinders are snakes that move by looping their bodies up in the air and pushing against the ground when they land. Their tracks look like a series of straight lines angling in the direction the snake was travelling.

Snakes do not wee. They secrete and excrete uric acid, which is a solid, chalky, usually white substance.

It takes about 50 hours for a snake to digest a frog.

The rock star Alice Cooper liked to wear a pet boa constrictor around his neck while on stage. One day, while Cooper was rehearsing in his hotel room, the snake started to constrict his neck. A bodyguard couldn't get the snake to release its grip, so he took out a penknife and cut off the snake's head.

The poisonous copperhead snake smells like freshly cut cucumbers.

Keen on knitting

Julia Roberts
Cameron Diaz
Russell Crowe
Uma Thurman
Winona Ryder
Goldie Hawn
Naomi Campbell
Julianne Moore
Kate Beckinsale
Sandra Bullock
Kate Moss
Ulrika Jonsson
Craig Charles
Geri Halliwell
Madonna
Hilary Swank
Sarah Jessica Parker
Rose McGowan

Famous people who have been featured on postage stamps

Sir Ian Botham – St Vincent

Arnold Schwarzenegger – Mali

Dolly Parton – Grenada

Eddie Murphy – Tanzania

Muhammad Ali – Liberia

Baroness Margaret Thatcher – Kenya

Barbra Streisand – St Vincent

George Michael – St Vincent

Robert De Niro – Gambia

Gary Lineker – Gambia

John McEnroe – Sierra Leone

Sir Mick Jagger – St Vincent

Sir Elton John – Australia

Aung San Suu Kyi – Gabon

Sir Winston Churchill – Germany

Dame Kiri Te Kanawa – New Zealand

Pure trivia

There are just two stations on the London Underground that have all five vowels in their names – Mansion House and South Ealing.

400 quarter-pound hamburgers can be made out of one cow.

Carnegie Hall in New York City opened in 1891 with Tchaikovsky as guest conductor.

The first ever World Summit on Toilets was held in Singapore in November 2001.

When left alone with a tea cosy, 98 per cent of men will put it on their heads.

The buzz generated by an electric razor in Britain is in the key of G. In America it is in the key of B flat.

Henry Ford was the man who started the Ford Motor Company but he never had a driving licence.

Popeye's friend Wimpy's full name is J. Wellington Wimpy.

Popeye's girlfriend Olive had a brother called Castor Oyl.

***Dracula* is the most filmed story of all time. *Dr Jekyll and Mr Hyde* comes second and *Oliver Twist* third.**

Oscars given out during the Second World War were made of wood because metal was in short supply.

Kleenex tissues were originally used as filters in gas masks.

Mel Blanc, the voice of Bugs Bunny, was allergic to carrots.

Traditionally, a groom must carry a bride over the threshold to protect her from being possessed by the evil spirits that hang around in doorways.

Apples are more effective at keeping people awake in the morning than caffeine.

Lipstick contains fish scales.

The monkey wrench was invented by Charles Moncke.

Opium was widely used as a painkiller during the American Civil War. More than 100,000 soldiers became addicts.

Eau de Cologne was originally marketed as a way of protecting yourself against the plague.

The Crystal Palace at the Great Exhibition of 1851 contained 92,900 square metres of glass.

In 1967 the American Association of Typographers made a new punctuation mark that was a combination of the question mark and an exclamation mark, and called it an interrobang. It was rarely used and hasn't been seen since.

After retiring from boxing, ex-world heavyweight champion Gene Tunney lectured on Shakespeare at Yale University.

215 pairs of jeans can be made with one bale of cotton.

About 10 million bacteria live in 1 gram of soil.

The record for finishing the Rubik's Cube is 16.5 seconds.

Pumpkins were once recommended for removing freckles.

Aoccdnrig to a rscheeacrh at Cmabgride Uinevrtisy, it deson't mtater waht oerdr the ltteres in a wrod are – so lnog as the frist and lsat ltteer are in the crorect pclae. Tihs is bcuseae we dno't raed ervey lteter but the wrod as a wlohe.

Harvard University's great rival is Yale University. Harvard uses 'Yale' brand locks on its buildings.

The tango originated as a (practice) dance between two men.

The quartz crystal in a wristwatch vibrates 32,768 times a second.

Gone with the Wind was set during the US Civil War but didn't feature a single battle scene.

Sharks

Sharks will continue to attack even when disembowelled.

Sharks are immune to all known diseases.

Sharks will eat anything except something in the vicinity of where they give birth. This is the only way nature prevents them from accidentally eating their own babies.

Females of some shark species give birth to only two young at a time.

Sharks have an additional sense that enables them to detect bioelectrical fields given off by other sea creatures and to navigate by detecting changes in the Earth's magnetic field.

The biggest egg in the world is laid by a shark.

Sharks have no bones. They consist of cartilage, muscle and teeth.

Lemon sharks grow a new set of teeth every two weeks. They grow more than 24,000 new teeth every year.

Whales

A killer whale, or orca, torpedoes a shark from underneath, bursting the shark by entering its stomach.

The killer whale is the fastest sea mammal. It can reach speeds up to 34 mph (56 kph) in pursuit of prey.

The orca is the largest member of the dolphin family.

Many large whales have a blowhole crest. This is an elevated area in front of their blowholes that stops water getting in while they're breathing.

At birth, the white whale is black.

Grey whales migrate 12,000 miles (19,000 km) each year.

A sperm whale's tooth is the size of a big peanut-butter jar.

Whales can die from pneumonia.

The grey whale has a series of up to 180 fringed overlapping plates hanging from each side of its

upper jaw. This is where teeth would be located if the creature had any.

Whales die if their echo system fails.

To change its line of sight, a whale must move its entire body.

A whale can swim for three months without eating.

A baby blue whale is 7.5 metres long at birth.

Humpback whales have an underwater song that evolves from year to year. Killer whales have individual songs which they rarely, if ever, change.

A baby baleen whale depends on a mother's milk diet for at least six months.

Because whales have such terrible breath, sailors believed at one time that a whiff of it could cause brain disorders.

Lasts

The last American Civil War veteran to die was John Salling, a Confederate soldier, who died in 1958 aged 112.

The last Horseman of the Apocalypse is Death, according to the Bible. (The Four Horsemen of the Apocalypse are Conquest, Slaughter, Famine and Death.)

The Beatles' last concert was at Candlestick Park, San Francisco, on 29 August 1966. The last song they played was 'Long Tall Sally'.

In 1921 John William Gott was the last person imprisoned for blasphemy in Britain.

The Beatles recorded their last song together, 'I Me Mine', in 1970.

The last song that Elvis ever performed publicly was 'Bridge Over Troubled Water', at his last concert in Indianapolis, in June 1977.

George Washington died on the last hour of the last day of the last week of the last month of the last year of the 18th century.

The last dodo bird died in 1681.